SOMERVILLE'S FORCE H

RAYMOND DANNREUTHER

THE ROYAL NAVY'S GIBRALTAR-BASED FLEET, JUNE 1940 TO MARCH 1942

First published in Great Britain
2005 by Aurum Press Ltd
25 Bedford Avenue, London WC1B 3AT

This paperback edition first published 2006

A catalogue record for this book is available from the British Library.

ISBN 1 84513 178 9

1 3 5 7 9 8 6 4 2
2006 2008 2010 2009 2007

Text design by Roger Hammond

Typeset by M Rules

Maps by Don Macpherson

Printed and bound in Great Britain by Bookmarque Ltd, Croydon, Surrey

The author and publishers are grateful to the Imperial War Museum, National
Maritime Museum and Royal Naval Museum for permission to reproduce
illustrations used in this book.

SOMERVILLE'S FORCE H

nond Dannreuther served as a midshipman in two ships of Force H, the
:oyer *Laforey* and the battleship *Malaya*. He ended the war as First
:tenant of a destroyer and then continued his career in the Royal Navy as
nnery specialist. He retired in 1972 with the rank of Captain, having
manded a battle-class destroyer, a frigate squadron and the guided missile
·oyer HMS *Glamorgan*. He died in March 2006.

Contents

Foreword by Admiral of the Fleet Sir Henry Leach GCB DL

FORCE H WAS a group of ships based at Gibraltar, operating uniquely under the direct control of the Admiralty and independent of any Commander-in-Chief. It was activated for some eighteen months in 1940–41. Principal among its multifarious tasks were maintaining the supply of aircraft and other essentials to beleaguered Malta, handling the French Fleet after the collapse of France, the *Bismarck* action, and the bombardment of Genoa.

The force was brilliantly led by Vice Admiral Sir James Somerville who had been invalided from the Navy before the war but, regaining full health, brought back on its outbreak. A true professional who had kept himself up to date with technological developments, he was a shrewd tactician, a charismatic commander and exactly the right man for the job.

The author, himself a distinguished Naval officer whose father fought at Jutland from the spotting top of the battlecruiser *Invincible* and was one of the six survivors from the ship, has narrated the many actions in which Force H participated with the accuracy of meticulous research and a skill which makes the reader feel he was there. You are inspired by the aggressive drive of the Force Commander. You are aghast at the contradictory muddle by the Admiralty over the handling of the French Fleet. You choke at the inane back-seat driving of Dudley Pound and Winston Churchill following the action off Spartivento. And you share in the exhaustion of being so constantly at sea under the toughest conditions of weather and enemy air attack – at one stage for fifty days out of fifty-six.

Force H has featured piecemeal in many other accounts of those times but no author has yet written the full story of the force. This book thus fills an important gap in the history of the Royal Navy in World War II. And it is grippingly readable.

Henry Leach
AF

Preface

the famous Force H, this new Fleet – for such it
became ...

STEPHEN ROSKILL, *THE WAR AT SEA*, VOL. I, P. 242

THE ROYAL NAVY squadron known as Force H operated from Gibraltar in the
early years of the Second World War. As a midshipman I served in two
ships in the force – the destroyer *Laforey* and the battleship *Malaya* – and I
chose it as the subject for a lecture I gave to our local military history group
a few years ago. When preparing the talk I was surprised to find that
although Force H featured prominently in many histories and accounts of
the war, no book had been published about it. Later, when researching the
present volume, I was intrigued by Admiral Somerville's comment, in his
report on the *Bismarck* action in May 1941, that although the Spanish,
German and Italian broadcasts referred to Force H, this designation was
never used in Admiralty communiqués about the force. In Britain's national
dailies at that time, it was described as 'a force from Gibraltar' or
'Somerville's Western Mediterranean fleet'. The title was released for publi-
cation two months later but received only scant mention when, shortly
afterwards, the loss of the force's best-known ship, the aircraft carrier *Ark
Royal*, was widely reported. There was little interest in Force H after the ship
had been lost, and in any case the use of the name lapsed a few months later.
There was evidently no general public awareness of the force during the first
year of its existence and little thereafter, even though in naval circles it was
well known and its title used freely. *Ark Royal* had become a household name
and the subject of a commemorative booklet issued by the Ministry of
Information in 1942. Her deeds, the subject of a number of books since
then, in many ways epitomised Force H and this may explain why the force
itself has not received attention.

In the event it was the historians who saved Force H from obscurity. Its
operations, mostly those already known to the public, were examined and

assessed, and the force structure in which they were carried out revealed. Its credibility was quickly established and its reputation became secure. But each of the operations on which it made its name lasted only a few days. For much of the time it operated out of the limelight and this can best be appreciated by referring to the full list of operations in Appendix 3. The purpose of this book is to give an overall account of all these operations so that the full story of the force can be told and its contribution to Britain's naval history better recognised.

There was no significance in the title Force H – there were in fact three forces of that name during the war. It was normal practice when ships were formed up for a particular operation that they should be controlled as a force, with a letter designation. In October 1939 eight hunting groups against German surface raiders, Forces F–N, were formed and Force H then consisted of two cruisers operating in the south Atlantic. Generally, as in that case, it was a short-lived commitment. The next Force H, formed at the end of June 1940 and the subject of this book, proved an exception and lasted until the end of March 1942. The book's title derives from Admiral Somerville, who commanded the force for all but its last three months. Six months later the third force of the name was reconstituted in different circumstances, as explained in the Epilogue.

Apart from my interest as a former member of the force, the impetus for writing this book has come from *The Somerville Papers*, published by the Navy Records Society in 1995. The collected reports and letters, edited by Michael Simpson, give a fascinating insight into the political intrigues and tribulations besetting the Commander of Force H, and some of the letters contain graphic eyewitness accounts of hostilities, often written within hours of the action. Augmented by extracts from official reports of proceedings and from other letters, there is the basis here for the story to be told of a remarkable force commanded by a remarkable man. Gratitude is due to Michael Simpson for illuminating this little piece of naval history to such good effect, and to the Navy Records Society for commissioning the work.

Much has been written about the better-known operations and little more remains to be said of them. I have aimed to tell the whole story of the force in a straightforward way to a wider audience, for the most part using contemporary records. Events are described in chronological order, which gives emphasis to the flexibility required of Force H in its operations, and Appendix 3 has been annotated to distinguish its Mediterranean and Atlantic activities. This flexibility is a theme which becomes evident in the story which follows, and is linked with two other consistent and interdependent themes: the way the composition of the force varied for different types of operation while remaining dependent on a permanent hard core of ships and the outstanding leadership provided by Somerville – all of which combined to give the force its special standing.

R. P. DANNREUTHER
November 2004

Glossary

AA	anti-aircraft
Asdic	Anti Submarine Detection Equipment Investigation Committee (of 1917), which gave its name to the equipment fitted in ships, later called sonar
ASV	airborne radar used to detect surface vessels
Axis	the alliance between Germany and Italy, joined later by Japan and other countries
boom	defensive net across harbour entrance
bulge	outer hull abreast main machinery spaces in capital ships to provide added protection
capital ship	battleship or battlecruiser
Captain	1 substantive rank in the Royal Navy between commander and rear admiral
	2 the Commanding Officer of a ship, whatever his rank
combing the track	altering course to align ship's course parallel to the track of a torpedo
crash barrier	restraining wires across a carrier's flight deck, raised before each plane lands to prevent it crashing into an aircraft parked on the fore part of the deck, and lowered immediately after landing to allow the plane to taxi forward to park
DF	Destroyer Flotilla
D/F	direction finding
E-boat	German fast motor torpedo boat
Enigma	coding device used for German naval communications
FAA	Fleet Air Arm
Flag Officer	officer of rear admiral's rank and above
Gosport tube	type of voice-pipe between pilot and observer
Levanter	prevailing (easterly) wind at Gibraltar for part of the year
longeron	longitudinal member of aircraft's fuselage
lower deck	the ratings who formed the ship's company
main body	ships in the centre of the formation being screened
MTB	motor torpedo boat

MT ships	merchant ships used to carry the Army's mechanical transport, including tanks
NAAFI	Navy, Army and Air Force Institutes
Oerlikon	Swiss-designed close-range 20mm AA gun
paravane	kind of kite fitted in larger ships for defence against moored contact mines. It was towed from the forefoot of the ship on either side, and its tow rope was intended to catch the mooring rope of a mine and slide the mine along it towards the paravane, preventing the mine swinging back towards the ship's hull and cutting the mine's mooring rope with wire cutters. Destroyers were not fitted with paravanes but some carried a comparable sweep, towed astern either side (TSDS), which cleared a path for heavier ships to follow
pom-pom	close-range AA gun firing 2-pdr shell
RDF	radio direction finding, later called radar
RNVR	Royal Naval Volunteer Reserve
schnorkel	air duct enabling U-boats to recharge batteries without surfacing
screen	escorting ships stationed ahead or around main body to provide anti-submarine and anti-aircraft defence
scuttle	1 porthole in ship's side 2 sink ship by opening seacocks
stick bombing	releasing bombs in quick succession
sub-calibre firing	firing ammunition of reduced calibre for practice purposes
TAG	Telegraphist Air Gunner
T/B	torpedo bomber
Their Lordships	the Lords Commissioners of the Admiralty, who together formed the Admiralty Board
throw-off firings	firings with full charge, the guns aimed off astern of the target ship
TSDS	two-speed destroyer sweep (see also *paravane*)
UP	Unrotated Projectile (rocket) used in air defence
VE Day	Victory in Europe Day, 8 May 1945
Vichy	French Government under Marshal Pétain after fall of France
V/S	visual signal

weather gauge	a sailing ship holding the weather gauge during battle is to windward (upwind) of her opponent, and thus able to dictate the course of the action
wireless or *W/T*	wireless telegraphy, later called radio
WRNS	Womens' Royal Naval Service

SOMERVILLE'S FORCE H

THE FORMATION OF FORCE H

THE STRATEGY

BRITAIN WENT TO war with Germany in September 1939. On 10 May 1940 Hitler launched his full offensive against the West. The evacuation of British and French forces from Dunkirk at the end of May was followed by the entry of the German Army into Paris on 14 June. Four days earlier Mussolini had declared war on the Allies Britain and France. On 22 June the Franco-German armistice was signed: three-fifths of metropolitan France would be occupied by the Germans; a collaborationist government based first in Bordeaux and later in Vichy and headed by Marshal Pétain would administer the unoccupied zone and the colonial Empire. And so collapsed all previous assumptions and strategies. The situation was entirely unexpected and new policies had to be decided immediately.

At that time Britain had an immense empire and the Royal Navy was a worldwide force. To look after the interests of Britain's Dominions and colonies, and to protect the Empire's trade and commerce, there were a number of naval bases around the world – in the Mediterranean at Malta and Gibraltar, and elsewhere at Bermuda, Simonstown in South Africa, Singapore and Hong Kong – and use could be made of the ports of the Dominion navies. There were two main fleets, the Home Fleet and the Mediterranean

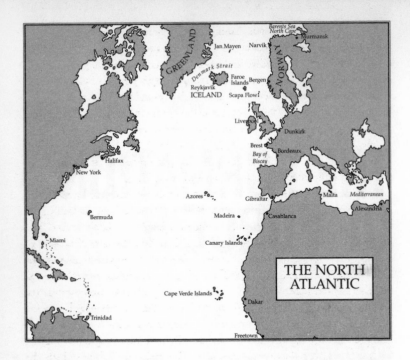

Fleet, each a composite force of battleships, aircraft carriers, cruisers, destroyers and other vessels. The wartime operating base of the Home Fleet was at Scapa Flow, and of the Mediterranean Fleet at Malta and at Alexandria in Egypt. At the other bases around the world a flag officer controlled his allotted area of ocean, with ships deployed to his region as circumstances required. Gibraltar was one such command, with a vice admiral commanding an area of the north Atlantic and a small part of the western Mediterranean.

One of the principles of pre-war policy agreed by France and Britain had been that in the Mediterranean the French would look after the western basin and Britain the eastern basin, with its fleet based at Malta and Alexandria. The first requirement now was to replace the lost French maritime power in the western Mediterranean and keep open the essential line of communications through those waters. The strategic importance of Gibraltar is self-evident, commanding as it does the narrow Straits (less than 10 miles wide) separating Europe from North Africa, and linking the Atlantic to the Mediterranean. A permanent force based there would secure the western gateway to the Mediterranean against hostile vessels, and also interdict French commerce to ensure it did not reach the enemy. From there attacks could be carried out on the Italian mainland. It was handily placed both to seize the Azores or Canaries if this proved necessary, and to defend them against attack. A naval force would help impress General Franco of Britain's continuing strength and determination, and deter Spain from joining the Axis powers of Germany and Italy. This was of great importance as Gibraltar would not be tenable if Spain became an enemy, and failure to guard the Straits might lead to the Italian fleet sailing into the Atlantic. A Gibraltar-based force would also be available to operate in the central Atlantic in defence of Britain's merchant shipping and in support of the Home Fleet. Such were the circumstances and assessments which led to the establishing at Gibraltar of Force H.

Italy dominated the central Mediterranean and put at high risk any ship on passage between the two British naval bases of Gibraltar and Alexandria. In the middle and about 1000 miles from each lay Malta, itself at risk. The Italian Navy's capability in 1940 was strengthened by the commissioning of the new battleships *Littorio* and *Vittorio Veneto* and the modernisation of two older battleships. There were in addition a number of cruisers with 8-inch and 6-inch guns and a powerful force of destroyers, torpedo boats and submarines. As long as a significant proportion of the French Fleet remained active in the western basin, Allied strength matched or outnumbered the Italian. But with France's defection the balance was now heavily in favour of the enemy, aided by Italy's commanding central position. The main ports from which the Italian fleet operated and which could influence Force H operations were Naples on the mainland, Messina and Augusta in Sicily, and Cagliari in Sardinia. There was a further threat from E-boats (fast motor torpedo boats) based at the island of Pantellaria. The Italian Air Force had airfields in Sicily and Sardinia. Except for a short strip of neutral Spanish Morocco opposite Gibraltar, the North African coastline was under the control of Vichy France, from which no assistance could be expected.

Westward from Gibraltar in the Atlantic, the nearest British bases were in the UK to the north and at Freetown in Sierra Leone, 1900 miles to the south. Northward from Gibraltar lay the neutral coastlines of Spain and Portugal, and German-occupied France. On that western seaboard Brest, France's pre-mier naval port, and Lorient, the first of the Biscay ports to be used as a U-boat base, gave the German Navy its foothold in the Atlantic. To the south between Gibraltar and Freetown the coastline was again Vichy controlled and contained the important ports of Casablanca and Dakar. The Atlantic islands – Azores, Canaries, Cape Verdes and Madeira – were Spanish or Portuguese owned and their neutrality had to be respected.

A Gibraltar-based force therefore would have to be capable of operating on two fronts: to the east in the Mediterranean, where the enemy had superiority in its surface and air forces; and to the west where the broad expanses of the Atlantic required long endurance steaming and a surface-action capability. In both seas there was a continuing threat of attack by submarine. To meet these requirements the composition of the force needed an aircraft carrier to provide air defence for the squadron, most important in the Mediterranean, a surface-strike capability and anti-submarine cover. Battleship support for the carrier was essential against the strong Italian battle fleet likely to be encountered in the Mediterranean and for offensive operations against ship or shore targets, and in the Atlantic to engage enemy surface raiders and provide cover for convoys, especially the troop convoys. And at all times there had to be an escort of destroyers, to serve as an anti-submarine screen and to provide an outer ring of AA (anti-aircraft) gunfire against air attack and a strike capability with their torpedoes and guns. Cruisers were bigger ships which could similarly provide protection to the main fleet units but which with their heavier armaments and longer endurance could be detached to patrol on their own or to carry out special missions.

THE SHIPS AND THEIR ARMAMENT

The names of many ships appear in this book. A brief introduction to the fleet that Britain had at the outbreak of war will help identify their role in operations.

Battleships

The Queen Elizabeth class (including *Warspite*, *Valiant*, *Barham* and *Malaya*) and the Royal Sovereign class (including *Resolution*, *Revenge*, *Ramillies* and *Royal Oak*) carried eight 15-inch guns. Both classes were built during the First World War, but only *Queen Elizabeth*, *Warspite* and *Valiant* had been extensively modernised and given a good AA armament. In the 1930s two ships *Nelson* and *Rodney*, each with nine 16-inch guns, joined the fleet.

Battlecruisers

These were battleships with 15-inch guns, some of whose protective armour had been sacrificed to give them their high speed of 30 knots compared to the 21–24 knots of the other battleships. Laid down during the World War I, they marked the final development of the large armoured cruiser concept that followed the revolutionary *Dreadnought* design. *Hood* was the largest of these at 42,000 tons with eight 15-inch guns; *Renown* and *Repulse* had three twin turrets.

Aircraft carriers

Ark Royal was the largest modern ship in the fleet. She had an armoured flight deck and two hangar decks. Older carriers, most of them converted from other hulls, were *Eagle, Courageous, Glorious, Hermes, Furious* and *Argus*.

Cruisers

There were various types of cruisers with 8-inch and 6-inch guns, the most numerous classes being the County class with eight 8-inch guns such as *Dorsetshire, Berwick* and *Suffolk*; and the modern Town class with twelve 6-inch guns such as *Sheffield, Manchester* and *Newcastle*, commissioned just before the war. Other older ships carrying 6-inch guns were the Arethusa and Danae classes and *Calcutta* and *Enterprise. Coventry* was rearmed as an AA cruiser with ten 4-inch guns.

Destroyers

The fleet destroyers were 30-knot ships. Successive flotillas of six to nine ships had names starting with the same letter of the alphabet. The A to I classes were armed with four 4.7-inch guns and eight torpedoes. A more powerful class of sixteen ships, the Tribal class including *Cossack, Gurkha* and *Sikh*, carried eight 4.7-inch guns in twin mountings, with additional AA armament and four torpedoes. They entered service shortly before the war, to be followed by the J to N classes carrying six 4.7-inch guns and eight or ten torpedoes.

By the end of June 1940, when the Force H story starts, the Navy had lost the battleship *Royal Oak*, the carriers *Glorious* and *Courageous*, three cruisers, twenty-three destroyers and twelve submarines. Two and a quarter million tons of merchant shipping had also been sunk. There was no period of 'phoney war' at sea during those early months of the war, as there was on land.

New ships from the Rearmament Programmes, started in the mid-1930s, began to join the fleet in 1940:

Battleships

The King George V class including *Prince of Wales, Duke of York, Anson* and *Howe* – fast ships of 29 knots with armour protection and ten 14-inch guns.

Aircraft carriers

The Illustrious class including *Victorious* and *Formidable*, with an armoured flight deck and one hangar deck. These were followed, all with armoured flight decks, by *Indomitable* with a lower half-hangar and later by *Implacable* and *Indefatigable* with full-length lower hangars.

Cruisers

The Colony class, such as *Fiji* and *Kenya*, with twelve 6-inch guns, comparable to the Town class but slightly smaller; and the Dido class of sixteen ships, such as *Euryalus* and *Hermione*, smaller ships carrying ten 5.25-inch guns.

Destroyers

The O to Z classes were flotillas of six to nine ships each with four 4.7-inch guns and eight torpedoes. The 4.5-inch gun was introduced in the newer C class which followed later. The Hunt class (*Avon Vale*, *Eridge* and so on) were smaller ships with a good AA armament of six 4-inch guns and of limited endurance and speeds, but which could be used as escorts for Malta convoys.

Other types of warship such as submarines, minesweepers and slower-speed frigates and corvettes used as convoy escorts do not feature in this résumé, which is concerned only with the types of ships with which Force H operated.

In 1940 the main weapons in the fleet were guns and torpedoes, still of conventional design but upgraded in performance over the years. Improvements in their control systems were still sought. Detection of submarines was by Asdic equipment, later to be called sonar, by which a pulse of soundwaves was sent through the water and reflected back to the ship on striking an obstruction. The equipment gave the direction and distance of the target but not its depth, so in any attack the level at which depth charges were set to explode had to be guessed. The most significant addition to the armoury was the introduction of RDF (radio direction finding), later to be called radar. Very few ships were fitted with this in the first year of the war. Initially the equipment at sea was in the metric band and provided air-warning cover. It could detect higher-flying planes out to a good range, but could offer only a rough estimate of height and was of little value for surface detection. For the latter, sets with shorter wavelengths in the 10cm band, the first in operation at sea in 1940, afforded greater precision and reliable ranges for gunnery fire-control systems. Later, 3cm band sets were still more precise and were capable of detecting periscopes, sea conditions permitting. The terms 'sonar' and 'radar' are used throughout this book.

The Fleet Air Arm's aircraft embarked in carriers were the Skua, a two-seater fighter–dive bomber, and the Swordfish, which were succeeded respectively by the Fulmar and Albacore. Unreliability and sometimes lack of voice communication made control of fighters cumbersome. Direction of these aircraft at that time required the range and bearing of aircraft detected by radar to be passed to *Ark Royal* (which was not fitted with radar) by flag hoist to avoid breaking W/T (wireless telegraphy) silence; this would be sent by Morse code to the observer in the fighter, who would calculate the course to intercept and pass it to the pilot by Gosport tube, a form of voice-pipe. No height information was available but this deficiency mattered less than it might, given that Italian Savoia SM 79s carried out high-level bombing attacks at about 13,000 feet, and that shadowers flew at zero feet or below cloud base.

Special prominence must be given to the Swordfish. An obsolescent biplane carrying an 18-inch aerial torpedo, it was Force H's main strike weapon, performing a torpedo bomber–spotter–reconnaissance role with a three-man crew. The telegraphist air gunner (or TAG), facing aft in the rear seat, also manned a Vickers gas-operated 0.303-inch machine gun. Communication was by Morse code, Aldis lamp or hand signal. The Swordfish was probably the last aircraft in service not to have an automatic cartridge starter; engines were ignited by two mechanics with a starting handle. It was a robust, reliable plane which could carry a great variety of stores and was a maid of all work. Its four-hour sortie could be extended up to six hours with an additional 'marathon' tank fitted in the observer's cockpit, displacing him to the more confined rear seat. Swordfish were known universally and with affection as Stringbags, the name deriving, so it is said, from old ladies' string shopping bags which could be expanded to hold more and more items. They were embarked in *Ark Royal*'s three squadrons, 810, 818 and 820. The RAF's long-range maritime patrol aircraft was the Sunderland, later succeeded by the Catalina.

When operating in shallower coastal waters, ships had to be protected against mines. For defence against moored contact mines the larger ships were fitted with paravanes (see Glossary). When the secrets of the magnetic mine, designed to lie on the sea bed and to be triggered by the magnetic field of a ship passing over it, were finally unravelled in November 1939, all ships were fitted with degaussing coils which neutralised the magnetic signature of the ship.

Force H was formed in great haste. Very soon after the Franco-German armistice had been signed in June 1940 three battleships, one carrier, two cruisers and attendant destroyers had assembled at Gibraltar. Its first task, the action at Oran, will be described in Chapter 3. After that operation had finally been concluded, part of the force returned to Britain. By 20 August its shape had become established and it remained essentially in that form for the next fifteen months. Other ships joined up for particular operations, but there was a permanent hard core which formed the basis of the force and which gave it its character and special spirit. The main units were the flagship, *Renown*, a battlecruiser with six 15-inch guns, modernised and with a good AA armament. Her fast speed made her a useful companion to *Ark Royal*. Indeed, before Force H was formed they had worked together in the south Atlantic looking for surface raiders. *Ark Royal*, with her aircraft, was the key unit of the force. From August 1940 to April 1941 she had thirty Swordfish, twelve Skuas and twelve Fulmars embarked, and thereafter thirty Swordfish and twenty-four Fulmars. Her AA armament consisted of eight twin 4.5-inch mountings, six eight-barrelled pom-poms and eight twin 0.5-inch machine guns. Before joining the force she had seen service in the Norwegian campaign. While hunting raiders in the south Atlantic with *Renown*, her aircraft had searched 4.5 million square miles of ocean. *Sheffield*, a cruiser carrying twelve 6-inch guns, was the only ship in the force to be fitted with air-warning radar. During the first winter of the war she had been worked hard, involving much steaming in northern waters. Christmas Day was spent patrolling the Iceland–Faeroes gap in the worst winter for forty years. Finally there was the 8th Destroyer Flotilla (DF) – eight ships of the F class with four 4.7-inch guns and eight torpedoes. The local destroyer flotilla based at Gibraltar, the 13th DF, joined up with the 8th DF, and vice versa, for operations with Force H or in the local area, as agreed between the two commanders, Flag Officer Force H, and Vice Admiral Commanding North Atlantic Station who was also the Flag Officer Gibraltar. The latter controlled a few minesweepers and armed boarding vessels. Further comments on the other ships that operated with Force H are given in Appendix 1.

THE ADMIRAL AND HIS STAFF

Vice Admiral Sir James Somerville was appointed to command Force H. Just before the war he had been invalided home from the East Indies with pulmonary tuberculosis. It was then a hard and fast rule in the Navy that anyone so diagnosed had to be discharged from the service, so although he had fully recovered by the time he got home he was compulsorily retired, to his great indignation. He was recalled one month later when war broke out. No ship was then fitted with radar and he was closely concerned with introducing it into the Fleet. During the Dunkirk evacuation he relieved Admiral Ramsay at Dover for short spells; and then three weeks later was sent to command Force H because he was immediately available and there was an urgent need to get the force established. He was known as a blunt, no-nonsense man, typical of a bluff seaman, with absolute clarity of purpose and the resolution to carry it out. He was not afraid to speak his mind to higher authority, and was intolerant of slackness or inefficiency within his squadron, an intolerance which he could express in colourful language. But he was a very human man with a zest for life and a great sense of fun, and he was well known for the humour in his signals. He had a good rapport with young officers and the lower deck, to whom he was known as 'Uncle James' or 'Our Jim'. The British public became aware of him early in the war in his regular BBC war commentaries, and were entertained by his asides, as when he remarked loudly, 'My God, they have given me water.' He knew the western Mediterranean well, having been the admiral commanding the Mediterranean Fleet destroyers during the Spanish Civil War in 1936–8.

Force H was unique in that it was not under the operational control of a commander-in-chief or an area commander. The Admiralty declared it to be a 'detached squadron' under Somerville's command. Despite the ambiguity in this description, which later became all too evident, Somerville was in no doubt that it was to be an independent command responsible directly to the Admiralty, and that it was not under the orders of Admiral Sir Dudley North, commanding the North Atlantic Station, who was senior to him and whose base at Gibraltar he was to use.[1] The two admirals were close friends who worked together in perfect harmony. Force H's presence in the western Mediterranean was of great significance to Admiral Sir Andrew Cunningham, Commander-in-Chief of the Mediterranean Fleet, whose effective operational area was now limited to the eastern Mediterranean, with the fleet based at Alexandria. He and Somerville had been cadets together and were good friends, and there was continual co-operation between them.

Force H was also a balanced force. Its considerable advantage was that the ships stayed together and could be worked up to an advanced state of efficiency. It had a commander who not only insisted on the highest standards but set them himself. He flew with the aircrews, who came to know that he appreciated their problems, a rapport that was to pay dividends later. Above all he was a modern admiral, who understood naval aviation and radar. The squadron was the first to develop air warning and fighter control with ship-fitted radars. A log of Force H operations is set out in Appendix 3 and may be referred to in connection with operations described in later chapters. Holders of key appointments in the force are shown in Appendix 2.

The number of ships that could join the force for a particular operation, some as big as a major fleet operation, gave Force H the status of a fleet for its operational activities. This was recognised in the size of the Admiral's staff. Normally the Admiral commanding a squadron would have his personal staff of secretary and flag lieutenant, the latter generally a signal officer, and for squadron duties would use the specialist seaman officers of the ship in which he flew his flag. Somerville's staff was on a larger scale. Besides his personal staff, he had a captain as chief of staff, two commanders for operations and plans, and seaman specialist officers specifically for Force H duties. The Secretariat included six paymaster lieutenants. Conditions were not easy for them. Not all battleships were fitted as fleet flagships which could accommodate large staffs, and the staff became accustomed to living rough, sometimes in curtained-off spaces in 'flats' in the after part of the ship. Nor was it a settled life for them: on one occasion they were told in *Renown* at 1.30 a.m. that they had two hours for the whole organisation to leave the ship. To begin with, they had a very difficult time. Somerville was intolerant of inertia and insisted on rapid action. But after six months he had trained his team to his satisfaction and he received in return a singular loyalty and devotion.[2] The unremitting stream of orders required for successive operations imposed a heavy burden on the staff, especially since different ships joined for different operations, often working with Force H for the first time and hence requiring comprehensive orders. The staff were gratified that, at a conference reviewing one major Malta convoy, admiration was expressed for the clarity of the orders.

FORCE H TERMS OF REFERENCE

Force H was formally constituted by signal from the Admiralty on 28 June 1940. The signal read:[3]

1. A detached squadron known as Force H under the command of Vice Admiral Sir James Somerville has been constituted as follows: HM Ships *Ark Royal*, *Hood*, *Resolution*, *Valiant*, *Arethusa*, *Faulknor*, *Foxhound*, *Fearless*, *Escapade*, *Forester*, *Foresight*.
2. The following ships will join Force H when they enter the limits of the North Atlantic Command: HM Ships *Nelson*, *Enterprise*, *Delhi*, *Fame*, *Fury*, HMC Ships *St Laurent*, *Skeene*
3. Force H will for the present be based at Gibraltar.
4. Subject to any instructions which may be given by the Admiralty the tasks of Force H will be
    a. to prevent units of the Italian Fleet breaking out of the Mediterranean
    b. to carry out offensive operations against the Italian Fleet and Italian coast.

Further tasks for the force were added later: the passage of reinforcements to the eastern Mediterranean; the control of the movements of all major units of the French Fleet; the hunting of the *Scheer* and other raiders in the Atlantic; offensive operations against the Spanish Fleet and harbours in the event of war with Spain; the capture of the Azores in certain circumstances; and the control of the Indian Ocean in certain other circumstances.

Somerville was also informed that the 13th Destroyer Flotilla would be placed at his disposal for any operations for which destroyers immediately under his command were not adequate; and that when Force H was in harbour the destroyers attached to it were to assist in the patrol of the Straits of Gibraltar as required by the Flag Officer Commanding the North Atlantic Station.

A few weeks after its formation Somerville concluded that Force H's most important task was 'the control of the Straits and that no other demands on the force, such as raiding the Italian coasts, should be allowed to endanger the fulfilment of this primary object, unless it was reasonably certain that such operations would be justified by the results likely to be achieved'.[4]

Later in the year the status of Force H and the Gibraltar command was reviewed. Consideration was given to upgrading the post of Flag Officer Commanding the North Atlantic Station (FOCNAS) to that of a commander-in-chief, but the idea was rejected. The new terms of reference were designed to meet the case of the Flag Officer Force H being either senior or junior to FOCNAS and were issued by the Admiralty by signal at the end of 1940:[5]

(a) The Flag Officer Commanding North Atlantic Station (FOCNAS) is responsible for preventing the passage of the Straits of Gibraltar by all enemy vessels and by vessels of other nations as may be ordered by the Admiralty from time to time;

(b) While Force H is based in Gibraltar the FOCNAS is to call upon the Flag Officer, Force H, for such assistance as may be necessary. Except when directed to carry out specific tasks by the Admiralty the Flag Officer, Force H, is to comply with such requests so far as he is able, but if, owing to conflicting claims, he is unable to do so, the Admiralty should be informed;

(c) Force H is available for operations in the Mediterranean as agreed to by the Admiralty and as mutually arranged by the Commander-in-Chief Mediterranean Station and the Flag Officer, Force H. It will be lent temporarily to the Mediterranean Station when so employed;

(d) The Flag Officer, Force H, remains responsible for the administration of Force H and its tactical deployment during operations, whether acting under the strategic control of the Admiralty, or Commander-in-Chief Mediterranean Station, or in compliance with a request from the FOCNAS.

It is interesting that no geographical limits of operation were imposed on Force H and that it was intended to be a free-ranging squadron able to operate under different authorities. The FOCNAS area of command extended only a few miles into the Mediterranean, over which the Commander-in-Chief Mediterranean exercised his control – as we have seen, for surface operations he was effectively restricted to the eastern Mediterranean east of the Sicilian Narrows, but he did maintain control of submarine operations throughout the Mediterranean. On no occasion was Force H lent to the Mediterranean Station for an operation, and Somerville's reports of proceedings were all made direct to the Admiralty. An exception was his report on the *Bismarck* action in May 1941, which was made to the Commander-in-Chief Home Fleet who was in operational control of the battle. And even though Force H operated more in concert with the Home Fleet than with the Mediterranean Fleet, as it did in the blockade of Brest in March–April of that year, the Admiralty retained control of the force and there was no arrangement for it to be lent to the Home Fleet.

LIFE AT SEA

War could be said to have imposed a new modus operandi on the Royal Navy of 1940, but much about its organisation continued as before. The Commander-in-Chief lived aboard his flagship, usually a battleship, with the fleet staff. Battleship, carrier and cruiser squadrons were commanded by a vice admiral or rear admiral with small staffs embarked. Senior captains commanded battleships, carriers and heavy cruisers, the more junior captains other cruisers and destroyer flotillas. Destroyers were commanded by commanders and lieutenant commanders, and sometimes by lieutenants.

The complement of a battleship and aircraft carrier was approximately 1500, of a cruiser 700 and of a destroyer 175. The three home ports, Chatham, Portsmouth and Devonport, besides providing dockyard facilities, were also the manning ports, and each rating was allocated to one of them. Ships were manned from the one port. Officers were appointed by the Admiralty from a general pool, with no home port affiliation. The peacetime commission of one to two years gave way to the operational requirements of wartime. Periodic refits or damage repairs generally determined the relief of crews, wholly or in part. Leave was given at these times or combined with shore training courses; and short spells of leave could be taken at boiler cleans or when the ship was at extended notice. Night leave was given when practicable. Mail to and from home was a major factor in maintaining morale. There was anxiety in both directions – that of the family at home about their man at sea; and in the ship on hearing on the BBC news of air raids on their home towns and cities, especially say in a Plymouth-manned ship when Plymouth was being blitzed. Censorship limited the postal address for all ships, worldwide, to 'c/o GPO, London'; there could be no reference to any particular fleet, force, squadron, flotilla or port. Mail if available was delivered to ships immediately on return to harbour. Outgoing mail was censored by the officers.

Officers lived in the after end of the ship in the Wardroom (for lieutenants and above), the Gunroom (for midshipmen) and in the Warrant Officers' mess. Officers had cabins; midshipmen slept in hammocks. In the forward part ratings lived in broadside messes and slept in hammocks; chief petty officers and petty officers had separate accommodation. Food brought from the galley was eaten on the mess decks. In destroyers the iron deck (the upper deck abaft the break of the fo'c'sle) could be awash in heavy seas, and lifelines with runners gave some help to officers making their way forward to the bridge to go on watch and sailors proceeding aft to man the guns and depth charges, and likely to get wet in the process. (In the R and later classes the Wardroom was moved to the forward part of the ship and ratings' accommodation and galley provided aft.) Movement inside the ship was restricted by the many bulkheads and hatches and doors; those on and below the waterline had to be closed by crew members after they had passed through. Depending on the threat at the time, varying measures were taken to limit damage from mines, torpedoes and air attack. Ventilation was by forced air trunking; there was no air conditioning. Scuttles (portholes) in the hull were kept closed at sea and ships were fully darkened overnight.

Each ship was a living community. Its effectiveness as a fighting unit required skilful management of the organisation, discipline and welfare of the ship's company to enable several hundred people to work and live together in a confined and uncomfortable environment for long periods. That statement could have been made at any time during the last few hundred years. One continuing legacy of those earlier centuries was the daily issue of a tot of rum to ratings over the age of eighteen who wanted it – half a gill neat for petty officers but watered down for other ratings.

The readiness of ships in harbour for sea was determined mainly by the time taken to flash up cold boilers and raise steam. Unless notified otherwise, ships reverted to four hours' notice on return to harbour. Generally this allowed shore leave to be granted. When shorter operational readiness was required, at two hours' notice boilers would have been warmed and ready to be brought into full operation. At one hour's notice or less, most boats would have been hoisted and the ship would be at very short notice to proceed. When requiring extended maintenance or repair periods in harbour, ships would revert to eight or twelve hours' notice.

At sea the flagship or the senior officer's ship would be the Guide of the Fleet, upon which other ships took up station according to the ranges and bearings appropriate to the formation ordered by the Admiral. Capital ships would be formed in line ahead, generally in single column but in two columns if there were sufficient number. The destroyers formed a screen ahead and on either bow of the main body, the number of escorts and the sonar operating conditions determining the disposition of the ships on the screen. The fleet's speed would rarely be less than 18 knots, unless restricted by weather or by the speed of a slower ship in company. Invariably the fleet would zig-zag as a method of defence against submarine attack. This involved alterations of course every five to twenty minutes of 10 to 60 degrees in different combinations set out in the zig-zag diagram book. The particular zig-zag was decided by the senior officer and depended on the degree of submarine threat, while taking account of the loss of speed in advance by not steering a steady course. Destroyers on the screen could operate their sonars at up to 23 knots. Above that speed the dome carrying the equipment under the hull had to be raised to prevent damage. If the fleet proceeded at high speeds, therefore, there would be no anti-submarine warning from sonar detections. But the high speed itself offered a measure of protection against torpedo attack. An aircraft carrier would take its place in the main body as a capital ship to be screened. Because of the need to steam into the wind when launching or recovering aircraft, the carrier had freedom to operate within the formation, keeping as much as possible within the area already swept by destroyers' sonars. Great importance was given to deck-landing training. In a well-worked-up squadron, successive planes could touch down only moments after the crash barrier (see Glossary) had been raised behind the previous aircraft, thereby greatly reducing the time the carrier was off-course from the rest of the fleet. If the wind came from astern the whole force might have to be turned round into the wind for flying operations, significantly reducing the speed of advance of the fleet. When escorting a convoy the capital ships would tuck themselves into the centre of the convoy between columns while the destroyers reinforced the escorts on the screen. Slow convoys were unlikely to zig-zag due to the severe impact this would have on their progress.

At sea ships were in a state of readiness for action depending on the threat at the time. Action stations were assumed on leaving harbour to bring all quarters to operational readiness before breaking down to a watchkeeping routine. Different ships had different arrangements but a common routine would be to have a part of the armament manned on a three-watch basis – four hours on and eight hours off except for the period from 4 p.m. to 8 p.m., which was split into two watches, called the 'dog watches', to ensure that men were not on watch for the same hours each day. Dawn action stations interrupted the cycle. Before radar was fitted, or became reliable for surface detection, ships had to be at immediate readiness for a chance encounter with the enemy at first light, when the horizon visibility greatly increased. In the Atlantic life at sea was mainly a matter of monotonous watchkeeping, enlivened by short spells of excitement when the enemy might be encountered. In more confined waters such as the Mediterranean where ships could be within easy bombing range from the shore, greater vigilance and readiness for action had to be maintained. Somerville's orders for a Malta convoy illustrate what this involved, and also demonstrate the fighting spirit he sought to inculcate in Force H:[6]

TO FORCE H AND SUBSTANCE CONVOY
20 July 1941

The main object of the operation on which we are now engaged is to pass a convoy of seven transports containing personnel and stores to Malta.

For over a year Malta has held out most gallantly against all assaults of the enemy. Until Crete fell we were able to supply Malta from both ends of the Mediterranean, but since the evacuation of Crete the situation has changed. For the present, Malta can only be supplied from the west and this is the task with which we have been entrusted.

To assist the achievement of our object every effort must be made to deny the enemy knowledge of our movements and intentions. This can be assured to a large degree if we

(a)   avoid making smoke, either from the boiler rooms or the galleys;

(b) use the lowest brilliancy lights for signalling, especially at dawn and dusk;

(c) take infinite care that no lights are visible at night;

(d) keep a very special look-out for the low-flying snooper that appears and disappears just on the horizon.

If the enemy detect our presence and attack with high level bombers, keep a special look-out for the very low-flying torpedo aircraft that may be attacking at the same time.

During this operation there will be long periods of first or second degrees of readiness. Everyone must make a point of taking rest and sleeping when not closed up, so as to be fresh and ready for action when required.

We must all of us have uppermost in our minds this one thought – the convoy *must* reach Malta. And it *will* reach Malta if every officer and man accepts his personal responsibility in ensuring the success of the operation and realises it's TEAM-WORK which does the job. Everyone must go full out, must key himself up for the maximum effort and not relax until the word is passed to 'stand easy'.

If the enemy attempts to stop us by surface, air or submarine forces, it is my intention to attack him and keep attacking him until he desists.

THE CONVOY MUST GO THROUGH!

GIBRALTAR

THE BASE PORT for Force H was Gibraltar, a rocky promontory only 2½ miles long from its southernmost tip, Europa Point, to the border with Spain. The Rock falls steeply to the sea on the Mediterranean side. On the west side lies the dockyard with the town running north–south along the lower sides of the Rock. A detached mole between two moles extending from the north and south ends of the harbour limited entrance to two 'gates', each protected by a boom. Ships could berth alongside and at buoys. The Rock provided shelter from easterly winds but the harbour was exposed to those from the west and south-west. There were three dry docks at the southern end of the harbour, the larger one extended to take a battleship in 1940, and a small dock next to the Yacht Club which could take a corvette (an escort vessel). Three capital ships could lie along the southern mole; the flagship *Renown* was normally berthed in the centre berth, the carrier *Ark Royal* in the south-east corner of the yard, the cruiser *Sheffield* alongside the Coaling Island or at head and stern buoys, and the destroyers in the pens at the northern end in the commercial part of the harbour. There were repair facilities for ships, and the dockyard could carry out seagoing repairs but only limited maintenance work.

The 'fortress of Gibraltar' lived up to its name. In 1940 in addition to the Gibraltar Regiment there were four battalions of infantry making up a garrison of 15,000 men. Over the years, and continuing during the war itself, tunnelling and excavations of the solid rock by the Royal Engineers had provided a labyrinth of defence works in which men, food, ammunition and essential services could be safely housed and operated under siege conditions. It was an impressive achievement.[1] Underground there was accommodation

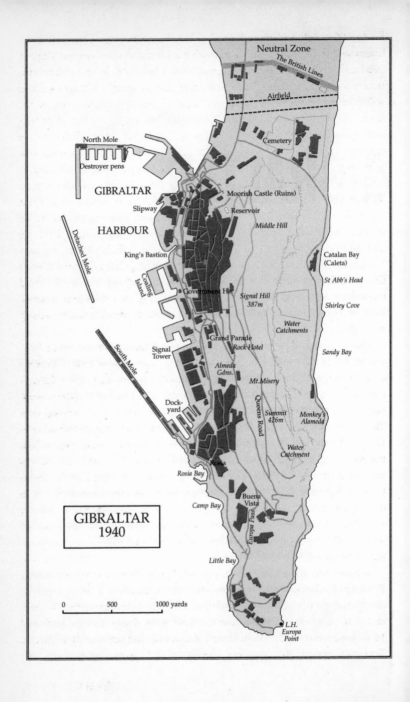

Neutral Zone

The British Lines

Airfield

Cemetery

North Mole

Destroyer pens

GIBRALTAR

Moorish Castle (Ruins)

Slipway

Reservoir

Middle Hill

HARBOUR

Catalan Bay
(Caleta)

St Abb's Head

King's Bastion

Coaling Island

Government Hse.

Signal Hill
387m

Shirley Cove

Water
Catchments

Sandy Bay

South Mole

Signal
Tower

Grand Parade

Rock Hotel

Almeda
Gdns.

Mt. Misery

Queens Road

Summit
426m

Monkey's
Alameda

Detached Mole

Dock-
yard

Water
Catchment

Rosia

Rosia Bay

Buena
Vista

Camp Bay

Europa Pass

GIBRALTAR
1940

Little Bay

0   500   1000 yards

L.H.
Europa
Point

for 16,000 people and enough food to last sixteen months. This included a bakery and frozen-food store, a generating station and telephone exchange, a 200-bed hospital, ammunition magazines and a large vehicle- and equipment-repair workshop, a water-distillation plant and substantial storage tanks to collect rainwater from the catchment areas on the steep eastern side of the Rock. The AA defences included 3.7-inch guns and the coastal battery of 9.2-inch guns. Initially Somerville was very critical of their efficiency. He considered that if a small proportion of the effort that had been expended on preparing the fortress against assault had been directed towards ensuring its use as a naval base, the AA defences would not have been in such a poor state. Tunnels were being drilled and caves excavated with quite remarkable zeal but the difficulties in installing UP projectiles and kite defences seemed to be insurmountable. But when Lord Gort arrived as Governor in April 1941, he and Somerville got on very well and the defences were futher improved. Saro London flying boats, later to be augmented by Sunderlands, part of 200 Group RAF, were moored in the north end of the harbour. The locally based naval force comprised the 13th Destroyer Flotilla of nine ships, and a patrol force of anti-submarine and minesweeping trawlers, armed boarding vessels and tugs.

Gibraltar was subject to four separate threats – from Germany, Spain, Italy and Vichy France operating from North Africa. In August 1940 Germany drew up plans for a full invasion, to be carried out in January 1941. Its capture would leave the way open for the Germans to occupy the Atlantic islands, particularly the Azores, and to move forces into North Africa to take over Vichy-controlled territories. The operation would require the co-operation of General Franco and the Spanish armed forces, and Spain would have to join the Axis. Franco however was not prepared to enter the war until he was convinced Britain was on her knees, and the action against the French Fleet at Oran in Algeria in July 1940 (see next chapter) was a determining factor in dissuading him. Germany made a further attempt to persuade Franco later in 1941, but the forthcoming invasion of Russia meant that the diversion of some 65,000 troops to capture Gibraltar was an impossibility, and all plans were abandoned.[2]

If Spain were to become hostile, geography put Gibraltar at a disadvantage. The town and dockyard on the west side of the Rock would be easy targets for the Spanish guns mounted the other side of the Bay. And the Straits, at their narrowest part next to the Mediterranean, were dominated by the 6-inch and 14-inch guns mounted in Ceuta on the south side, and between Algeciras and Tarifa on the north side. Two further 6-inch guns mounted on the

Mediterranean coast a few miles north of Gibraltar could reach targets on the northern and some of the eastern sides of the Rock.[3] The airfield at North Front, right on the border with Spain, ran east–west across the narrow isthmus joining the Rock to the mainland. Before the war it had been the racecourse and a grass field; *Ark Royal*'s aircrews helped to demolish the grandstand. This was politically sensitive land, and initially there was agreement with Spain that it could be used for the training of naval aircraft and for their maintenance. Strict flying instructions for taking off and landing were issued and pilots were warned that the Spanish made a practice of firing at aircraft infringing their air space. The airfield was very vulnerable and if Spain did enter the war it would become untenable. If that should happen there was a proposal to build runways on Europa Point, similar to flight decks with accelerators and arrestor wires, for use by Hurricanes. But the RAF could not spare the fighters and the scheme was taken no further.

The Italian threat came from occasional air raids but more significantly from their two-man torpedoes. Launched from a parent submarine, these were fitted with a detachable warhead which was to be placed under a ship's hull. At the end of October 1940 one of these craft successfully negotiated the boom across the harbour entrance but hit bottom before reaching its target, the battleship *Barham*, and its attack failed.[4] Patrols by ships' boats were reinforced, supplemented later by Fairmile motor launches. A further attack by three Italian units in May 1941 was likewise unsuccessful, but in September that year another attempt was more effective, and later in 1942 merchant ships in Gibraltar Bay were attacked. After the Italian armistice the following year it was found that a scuttled tanker off nearby Algeciras had been used as a secret base. The more immediate and readily felt threat was the spasmodic bombing by Vichy French aircraft from their North African bases. In the main these consisted of retaliatory raids after a naval incident.

When France was on the point of collapse in May 1940, the Gibraltar authorities ordered an immediate evacuation of women and children, and of all non-combatants not involved in essential services. A few returned to England but the majority crossed the Straits to French Morocco. When France fell there was a hasty re-evacuation from Morocco back to Gibraltar and thence to the United Kingdom and elsewhere. About 13,000 Gibraltarians left the Rock. The domestic crisis this caused was solved by NAAFI setting up communal restaurants to cater for 6000 people; and by the employment as housekeepers of some of the hundreds of Spanish women who, because the border with Spain had stayed open, crossed the frontier each morning to work on the Rock and leave again in the evening. Every morning there was also a

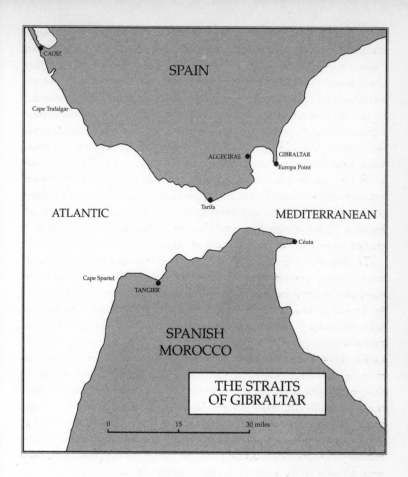

CADIZ

SPAIN

Cape Trafalgar

ALGECIRAS

GIBRALTAR
Europa Point

ATLANTIC

Tarifa

MEDITERRANEAN

Céuta

Cape Spartel

TANGIER

SPANISH
MOROCCO

THE STRAITS
OF GIBRALTAR

0   15   30 miles

convoy of mule carts trundling across the frontier laden with fruit and veg-
etables. And visits could be made to local towns, including Algeciras and La
Linea, where there was a bullring, though service personnel had to return by
4.30 p.m. A strict curfew was enforced from 9.00 p.m. in Gibraltar. It was very
much an all-male society and the only women remaining on the Rock after
the evening curfew were the handful of Women's Royal Naval Service and
nursing staff in the hospital. The Gibraltar Wrens were one of the first of the
women's services to be sent overseas. The ship bringing out the first draft, SS
Aguila, was torpedoed and sunk off the Azores in August 1941. Most of the
twenty-two Wrens were lost, but some were picked up only to be torpedoed
again three nights later. None survived to reach Gibraltar.[5]

Life on the Rock was said to resemble life in a battleship – that of a self-contained masculine community dependent on itself for all amenities, amusements and survival. But in many ways Gibraltar was an attractive place to be based during the war. Compared to the bleakness of Scapa Flow, it offered a more civilised welcome on return from sea. There was no blackout; there were shops, cinemas and canteens ashore and games facilities. Along Main Street shops, pubs and girlie bars plied their trade. Silk stockings, perfume and chocolates, luxury wartime presents, were available to take home. There was always a plentiful supply of local red wine from Spain and Morocco; sixpence would buy a pint of port and lemon. But beer had to come from the UK and occasionally the requirements of the 20,000–30,000 men on the Rock could not be met – although Somerville was quick to report any shortage. A small supply of onion beer could be obtained from Spain but it was not very palatable. The weather could be unkind, ranging from full gales to the Levanter, a liverish easterly wind that provided a curtain of cloud on the top of the Rock and could last for days. But mostly the weather was warm and reasonable, hot in the summer, and there were none of the bitterly cold and unpleasant conditions experienced in the north Atlantic. A half-mile tunnel from the dockyard led through to Sandy Bay in the Mediterranean, where the water for bathing was 10 degrees warmer.

The downside to being at Gibraltar was that there was little scope for relaxation. In due course, when men had experienced all the facilities on offer in the confined area of the Rock, boredom could set in, and it was then that they really felt the lack of opportunity for leave. In Home Fleet ships the home ports were 'just around the corner' and boiler cleans or short refits allowed some leave to be given, if only for a few days. Somerville's ships were often in the news: they got the glamour but not the leave. Crews of Home Fleet ships joining Force H for operations always declared that they would prefer the leave option. Nevertheless the men in the force had a strong sense of pride in their ships and in the knowledge that every time they sailed into the Mediterranean there was a real possibility they would be in action against the enemy.

While Gibraltar was ideally situated for operations in the Mediterranean and the Atlantic, its immediate surroundings posed a security problem. The town and dockyard are on the west side of the Rock, and across the Bay of Gibraltar to the west, only 4½ miles distant, lies Algeciras. Because of its proximity and the excellent view it provided, this Spanish town was home to many German and Italian agents. With powerful binoculars they could easily monitor not only movements of shipping into and out of the harbour, but also to some extent what went on inside the harbour. Precautions had to be taken. There were various forms of deception on sailing. For an operation in the Mediterranean, Force H might sail in the afternoon west into the Atlantic, and when out of sight of land reverse course, pass through the Straits at night and be out of sight in the Mediterranean before daylight. There could be variations on this: a force might sail in two halves, one half going east, and the other west before doubling back at night; or a convoy bringing supplies for Gibraltar might go through the Straits at night and arrive next day as if it had come from the east. On one occasion a dummy convoy was sailed east into the Mediterranean, reversing course later to arrive back in Gibraltar during the night. All these deceptions were intended to sow doubt and mislead. Account also had to be taken of the numerous fishing vessels always present in the Straits. It had to be assumed that their crews were paid to report warship movements. When troops were being brought to Gibraltar in preparation for a Malta run, special instructions were given to limit the number appearing on deck.

It was from Gibraltar that Force H, within days of its formation, launched one of the most decisive operations of the war: the action at Oran.

3

THE ATTACK ON THE FRENCH FLEET

FROM THE MOMENT the French Government sought an armistice with Germany in the summer of 1940, the immediate concern for Britain's Prime Minister Winston Churchill was the possibility of France's powerful Fleet, Europe's second largest, falling under German control. The Franco-German armistice came into effect on 24 June and obliged the French Government under Marshal Pétain to prevent their Fleet falling into British control, and to demobilise and disarm the ships. But there could be no guarantee that Hitler would respect the treaty and not take over the vessels. On 12 June Admiral Darlan, the French Naval Chief, had assured Churchill that there would be no question of surrendering his Fleet – 'it would be contrary to our naval tradition and honour'. Six days later he had given a personal promise to A. V. Alexander, the First Lord of the Admiralty, and to Admiral of the Fleet Sir Dudley Pound, the First Sea Lord, who had flown to Bordeaux to see him, that the French Fleet would never surrender to the enemy. But Darlan then joined Pétain's cabinet, thereby identifying himself with the Vichy regime and throwing doubt on his commitment to those earlier promises. The British Admiralty expected the French to argue that they would scuttle if the Germans or Italians attempted to seize their ships, even in French metropolitan ports. But with the French Army disarmed, and the Fleet laid up with reduced crews under German and Italian surveillance, there could be no certainty that, however resolute the attempt to destroy or sink any particular ship, it would be possible to forestall seizure by the enemy.[1]

A number of ships had already been taken to British ports. There was a French squadron at Alexandria and at Mers-el-Kebir, a small port on the Algerian coast 3 miles west of Oran; and also some vessels at Oran itself and Algiers. These included well-armed cruisers and destroyers, including at Mers-el-Kebir the *Dunkerque* and *Strasbourg*, formidable new battlecruisers carrying eight 13-inch guns. If they fell into German or Italian hands they could well turn the naval balance in Europe against Britain. On 23 June Admiral North was sent in the destroyer *Douglas* from Gibraltar to put the Government's proposals to Admiral M. B. Gensoul commanding the French squadron at Mers-el-Kebir. Gensoul was distressed by the possibility of a split with Britain, but he felt that the French had to abide by the terms of the armistice agreement. He assured North that although he could not turn over his ships to the Royal Navy the Germans would not get them, and that he had made arrangements to blow their bottoms out if there were any attempt to do so. But if Britain attacked his ships they would fight their way to their home port.[2]

Urgent discussions now took place in London. It was decided that Somerville with Force H should present an ultimatum to Gensoul, giving him four options: to sail and join Britain; to sail with reduced crews under British control to a British port, the crews being repatriated and, for both these options, the ships being returned at the end of the war with compensation for any damage inflicted in the interim; to sail with reduced crews to French ports in the West Indies where they would be demilitarised and the crews repatriated; or fourth, if these offers were refused, to sink their ships within six hours. If Gensoul declined all of these options and instead suggested that the ships be demilitarised in their present berths, this could be accepted. But Somerville first had to be satisfied that the necessary measures could be carried out under his own supervision within six hours, and that they would be enough to prevent the ships being brought into service for at least one year in a fully equipped dockyard port. Otherwise his instructions were emphatic: the ships were to be destroyed, especially the *Dunkerque* and *Strasbourg*, by all means at his disposal.[3] The destroyers and submarines at Oran were also to be sunk, provided that could be done without considerable loss of civilian lives, but the French cruisers at Algiers could not be attacked without causing such loss and indeed destroying the town. The operation was to be co-ordinated with other actions elsewhere against the French Fleet. The chosen date was 3 July and the operations had to be completed during daylight hours on that day. Two submarines would be deployed to report any French ship movements, but they were not to attack.

Somerville arrived in Gibraltar on 30 June and hoisted his flag in *Hood*. In preliminary discussions with Admiral North, Vice Admiral L. V. Wells commanding the Aircraft Carrier Squadron in *Ark Royal*, and Captain C. S. Holland, Captain of *Ark Royal*, all were strongly opposed to the use of force and believed there was little reason to fear that the French would allow their ships to fall into German hands. Their views were represented to the Admiralty. On 2 July Somerville held a meeting of flag and commanding officers to explain and discuss the operation. Holland, who had recently served as naval attaché at the British Embassy in Paris and knew the French well, would be Somerville's emissary to the French Admiral, handing over command of his ship meanwhile to his Executive Officer. He would proceed ahead of the force in the destroyer *Foxhound*. There was no plan to lay mines except as a last resort, because their presence in the water would prevent the French from accepting the peaceful options and would also render impossible the entrance of the British destroyers with demolition parties. If necessary, aircraft could be armed with mines at short notice. It was hoped that the action taken at Mers-el-Kebir would induce the French to scuttle their ships at Oran.

Later that day Force H sailed: three battleships (*Hood*, *Valiant*, *Resolution*); the aircraft carrier *Ark Royal*; two cruisers (*Arethusa* and *Enterprise*) and eleven destroyers. In the evening the force was attacked by a submarine, a torpedo exploding ahead of the destroyer *Vortigern*, but no detection was made. That night Churchill asked the Admiralty to signal Somerville, 'You are charged with one of the most disagreeable and difficult tasks that a British Admiral has ever been faced with, but we have complete confidence in you and rely on you to carry it out relentlessly.'[4]

In the course of the following day, 3 July, there was much signalling between Somerville and London, Churchill remaining in the cabinet room for most of that time in frequent contact with the Admiralty. Somerville's official report on the action gives us a clear picture of what happened.[5]

At 0620 the French authorities at Mers-el-Kebir were asked to permit *Foxhound* to enter the port and at the same time a signal (in French) was sent to Admiral Gensoul:

The British Admiralty have sent Captain Holland to confer with you. The British Navy hope their proposals will enable you and your glorious French Navy once more to range yourselves side by side with them. In these circumstances your ships would remain yours and no one need have anxiety for the future. A British Fleet is at sea off Oran waiting to welcome you.

Permission to enter was received at 0742 and the ship was met by a pilot with instructions to proceed inside Mers-el-Kebir and to berth near *Dunkerque*. On the pretext that messages might have to be conveyed to Somerville and as a precaution against being prevented from sailing, *Foxhound* instead anchored 1½ miles outside the harbour at 0800. Gensoul sent his Flag Lieutenant to inform Holland that the Admiral was unable to see him but he could meet his Chief of Staff. At 0847 Holland embarked in *Foxhound*'s motor boat. He was met halfway between the inner boom and the breakwater by the Flag Lieutenant in the Admiral's barge. Holland handed him Britain's ultimatum and said he would wait for a reply. The ultimatum concluded with the warning that, if it was rejected, force might be used to prevent the ships falling into German or Italian hands.

At 0910 Force H arrived off Mers-el-Kebir. In case Gensoul tried to conceal the alternative proposals from his officers and men, Somerville directed *Hood*, *Valiant*, *Resolution*, *Arethusa* and *Enterprise* to flash by signal projector to the French heavy ships the message (again in French): 'For Admiral Gensoul from Admiral Somerville. We hope most sincerely our proposals will be acceptable and that we shall have you on our side.' At 1000 the Flag Lieutenant returned with a written reply confirming Gensoul's earlier response to Admiral North: French warships would not be allowed to fall intact into the hands of the Germans or Italians. The note added that 'in view of the meaning and form of the veritable ultimatum which has been sent to him, French warships would meet force by force'. Holland had a long and friendly conversation with the French Flag Lieutenant, who returned to *Dunkerque* at 1050 with a written statement prepared beforehand. In reply Gensoul's Chief of Staff brought out a written reply reiterating the Admiral's previous statements, declaring that he had decided to defend himself by every means possible; and pointing out to Somerville that the first shot fired would have the immediate effect of putting the whole French Fleet against Great Britain, a result diametrically opposed to what HM Government wished to achieve.

All this time Force H was steaming to and fro across the Bay and making occasional legs to seaward. Ships' companies were at action stations but guns kept trained fore and aft; paravanes were streamed. The upperworks of the French battleships, which were anchored with their sterns to the mole, were clearly visible over the breakwater. Reconnaissance aircraft from *Ark Royal* had earlier reported that these battleships and the cruisers were raising steam and that awnings over the deck were being furled. At 1045 the Admiralty signalled Somerville that magnetic mines could be laid to stop the ships from leaving harbour. Holland returned onboard *Foxhound* at 1125, to be told by Somerville that it was imperative that the French should know that they would not be allowed to leave harbour unless the British terms were accepted. The message was passed to the Flag Lieutenant at 1140. At the same time a message was passed to Gensoul by light informing him of the action being taken by his counterpart at Alexandria, Admiral Godfroy, to demilitarise his ships. Despite this, Somerville received a summary of Gensoul's written reply at 1227, indicating the apparent intention of the French ships to put to sea and fight. He ordered the entrance to the port to be mined and reported to the Admiralty that he was preparing to open fire at 1330. At 1307 minelaying aircraft were flown off with fighter escort and five mines laid in the entrance to the harbour. Shortly afterwards an aircraft reported that the boom, which had been opened, was now closed and ships' boats had not yet been hoisted. As it appeared that the French had no immediate intention to head out to sea, Somerville elected to give them until 1500 to reach a decision.

At 1340 *Foxhound*, in visual touch with *Dunkerque*, was directed to instruct Gensoul to hoist a large square flag at the masthead if he accepted the British terms. Gensoul signalled at 1440 that he was ready to receive a delegate for honourable discussion. Holland embarked in *Foxhound*'s motor boat at a point north of the harbour and clear of the minefield. This involved a passage of 7½ miles and it was not until 1615, after transferring to the Admiral's barge inside the harbour, that he arrived onboard *Dunkerque*. All the French ships were in an advanced state of readiness for sea, control positions manned, and tugs standing by the stern of each battleship. Holland was received very formally by Gensoul in the Admiral's cabin. The Admiral was indignant about the ultimatum and about the mining of his harbour. It was apparently only after considerable discussion that he began to understand that fire might really be used.

At 1646 the Admiralty, having intercepted French signals traffic, instructed Somerville to settle matters quickly or he would have to deal with French ships on their way from Algiers to reinforce Gensoul. He immediately signalled Gensoul visually and by wireless that if the terms were not accepted fire would be opened at 1730. The message reached Gensoul at 1715, while he was still conferring with Holland. A brief signal was sent in reply stating that the French crews were being reduced and the ships would proceed to Martinique or the USA if threatened by the enemy. Holland finally left *Dunkerque* at 1723; at the same time 'action stations' were sounded in French ships. Somerville received the signal at 1729 but, as it did not comply with any of the conditions laid down, Force H prepared to take decisive action: air striking forces were flown off and the battleships stood in to the coast.

Hood, *Valiant* and *Resolution* opened fire with their 15-inch guns at 1754, at maximum visibility range of 17,500 yards with aircraft spotting. The line of fire was from the north-west, ensuring not only that fire from the French ships was to some extent blanked by Mers-el-Kebir fort but also that damage to civilian life and property was reduced. After firing thirty-six 15-inch salvoes fire was ceased at 1804 to allow the French to abandon their ships and to avoid further loss of life. In those ten short minutes, the battleship *Bretagne* had blown up; the battleship *Provence* and the battlecruiser *Dunkerque* had run aground; the seaplane carrier *Commandant Teste* had caught fire; and one destroyer had been crippled. A total of 1299 French sailors had been killed, 930 in *Bretagne* alone, and another 350 wounded. The shore batteries had opened fire about a minute after the first British salvo, and were engaged by *Arethusa*. A number of main armament projectiles from the French ships fell close to Force H ships, in some cases straddling them (that is, falling both short of and beyond them). There were no hits but splinters caused minor damage in *Hood* and injured one officer and a rating. In one destroyer which was straddled, an unexpected hazard was the dye used by the French to distinguish splashes of their fall of shot, causing white uniforms to turn green. As fire from the forts became increasingly accurate, the British ships altered course away and made smoke. They sailed westward to take up a position from which further bombardment of the French ships could be carried out if necessary, without causing casualties to men struggling ashore in boats or exposing Force H unduly to fire from the forts. The force received repeated signals from shore visual and wireless stations asking that fire be stopped, to which the reply was sent: 'Unless I see your ships sinking I shall open fire again.'

The explosion of the *Bretagne* produced an immense column of smoke several hundred feet high. Together with the smoke from several other fires burning among the French fleet, this made observation difficult. At 1830 reports confirmed the escape of the battlecruiser *Strasbourg* and five destroyers to the eastward. *Hood*, accompanied by cruisers and destroyers, gave chase. Six Swordfish armed with 250lb bombs, already airborne with Skua escort for an attack on the heavy ships in harbour, were redirected to attack. It was well pressed home and met with heavy opposition, but there were no hits. Two Swordfish failed to return, their crews being picked up by *Wrestler*. A further attack on *Strasbourg* by six Swordfish, armed with torpedoes, was made at 2055 shortly after sunset; one explosion was seen under the stern and a possible hit reported amidships. No aircraft were lost. The pursuing ships steamed on at full speed until 2020 when the chase was abandoned. At that point *Strasbourg* and the destroyers were 25 miles ahead of *Hood* and it was estimated that the Algiers force, which included several 8-inch and 6-inch cruisers, would meet *Strasbourg* shortly after 2100. A night action was not considered justified against this numerically superior force when the prospects of locating and engaging the French battlecruiser were small. Fire was opened on French reconnaissance and bombing aircraft between 1930 and 2100. The few bombs dropped fell wide and no attacks were pressed home. The *Strasbourg* eventually returned to Toulon, in Vichy-controlled France.

It was intended to fly off a strike of twelve Swordfish and nine Skuas at 0400 the next morning, but there was thick fog and the attack had to be abandoned. When Gensoul informed Somerville that his ships were *hors de combat* and that he was ordering personnel to evacuate their ships, Force H withdrew and returned to Gibraltar, securing alongside by 1900 on 4 July.

The force, without *Resolution*, sailed again next day to carry out a second attack on *Dunkerque* at Mers-el-Kebir. Somerville persuaded the Admiralty that a bombardment would mean further loss of life among French sailors and also among civilians as the town was close by. A torpedo attack was authorised instead and carried out early on 6 July. Six or seven hits were obtained which put the ship out of action until early 1942, when she likewise returned to Toulon.

In the final part of his report Somerville speculated:[6]

whether the use of fire might not have been avoided had Gensoul agreed to meet Holland in the first instance. The final offer made by the French Admiral was very near to a British alternative but differed, unfortunately, in the proviso that the action proposed would not be carried into effect *unless* there was a danger of the French ships falling into the hands of the enemy. Gensoul claimed that this danger was not imminent; we maintained that it was. I believe that given more time Holland might have succeeded in converting Gensoul to our point of view. At the actual time when the latter made his offer, it was already too late, since French reinforcements were approaching and the orders of HM Government were explicit that a decision had to be reached before dark.

Somerville was congratulated by the First Lord and First Sea Lord on the results so far achieved and on the efficiency of the bombardment, compliments with which the Prime Minister associated himself. For Churchill it was his most decisive action during the first weeks when Britain stood alone. For Somerville it was a hateful business. He wrote, 'we all feel thoroughly dirty and ashamed that the first time we should have been in action was an affair like this', and he blamed himself for having let the *Strasbourg* escape. To his wife he declared, 'If I didn't feel that in war one can have only one loyalty and that is to King and Government I shouldn't hesitate to ask to be relieved at once.' Holland in fact did ask to be relieved of his command of *Ark Royal* but was persuaded to withdraw the request. But while to the senior officers it was all 'simply incredible and revolting', Somerville reported that it did not seem to worry the sailors at all and there were conflicting opinions in the ships. This was noted in *Valiant*:[7]

During the delay in opening fire while Somerville argued with the Admiralty, a distinct division was evident on board. The older officers who had previous contact with the French Navy, shared the Admiral's qualms. Junior officers and certainly the Ship's company wanted to get on with it (it was evident that the French ships were raising steam and preparing for sea – furling their awnings and hoisting boats). This attitude probably represented more accurately the opinion of the British public, who believed rightly or wrongly that France had let her ally down and was changing sides.

In the immediate aftermath of what the British called the Oran action and the French Mers-el-Kebir, there were harsh thoughts in London: 'Never had anything been seen comparable to the two nations who had so recently been allies now fighting while the barbarians sat back and laughed.' Churchill remarked that 'the French were now fighting with all their vigour for the first time since war broke out'. Nor did he see how Britain could avoid being 'at war with France tomorrow'.[8]

Not surprisingly, the French casualties generated great resentment and bitterness in France, echoes of which have not faded more than sixty years later; and there was a an angry reminder of the past when the blowing up of the *Bretagne* was likened to that of *L'Orient* in Nelson's action at the Battle of the

Nile further along the coast. Vichy loudly proclaimed Britain's perfidy and North Africa confirmed its allegiance to France. Resistance was virtually guaranteed to the Allied invasion of North Africa in November 1942, and to other raids against French territories. And Gibraltar became a target for Vichy bombers.

Churchill saw the action as an overriding necessity. It was vital to show the world that Britain was determined to continue to fight, and was not down and out as so many thought after Dunkirk. It was especially important that Spain and the United States should see Britain's resolve – Spain because she was wobbling and might easily join the Axis; the US because Britain was currently negotiating to obtain fifty destroyers which were essential for convoy escort until her shipbuilding programme could produce the ships that were so desperately needed, and America – not least President Roosevelt – was sceptical about Britain's ability to survive.

The BBC claimed that there was widespread public support for the action. Spain was in fact much impressed and remained neutral, resisting pressure to take the Axis side and co-operate in German plans to capture Gibraltar. Roosevelt and the American public were now convinced that Britain would fight on, and the destroyers were handed over. Six months later, in January 1941, Churchill is recorded as saying that 'he believed Oran had been the turning point in our fortunes; it made the world realise that we were in earnest in our intention to carry on'.[9]

In *Their Finest Hour*, the second volume of his Second World War memoirs, Churchill devoted one chapter exclusively to Oran, entitled 'Admiral Darlan and the French Fleet, Oran'.[10] Churchill regarded Darlan, whose great-grandfather had been killed at the Battle of Trafalgar, as one of those good Frenchmen who hate England. The French Navy was fiercely loyal to the Admiral and would have obeyed his order to leave French ports to avoid seizure by the Germans. And he was ready to give that order until he joined Pétain's cabinet. When asked why he had changed his mind, he replied, 'Because I am now Minister of Marine.' Churchill lamented that if only Darlan had led the French Fleet away, he would have achieved all the honour and fame he sought, he would have become the chief of the French Resistance; and nothing could have prevented him becoming the Liberator of France. Instead he went forward to ignominious office, a violent death by assassination, a dishonoured grave and a name long to be execrated by the French Navy. Churchill likened it to a Greek tragedy. He ended the chapter with this tale told him by a member of the Resistance movement who later became Minister of Defence:[11]

In a village near Toulon dwelt two peasant families, each of whom had lost their sailor son by British fire at Oran. A funeral service was arranged to which all their neighbours sought to go. Both families requested that the Union Jack should lie upon the coffins side by side with the Tricolour, and their wishes were respectfully observed. In this way we may see how the comprehending spirit of simple folk touches the sublime.

One feels Churchill drew some comfort from that story.

In the other operations against the French Fleet on 3 July, in the early hours of the morning there was a successful outcome at Portsmouth where the ships were taken over, but at Plymouth two officers (both British) and two ratings (one British and one French) were killed when the submarine *Surcouf* was boarded.[12]

In Alexandria the Commander-in-Chief of the Mediterranean Fleet Admiral Sir Andrew Cunningham had established good relations with Admiral Godfroy, the Admiral of the French squadron, during the previous three months. Negotiations were going well until Godfroy received news of the bombardment and loss of life at Mers-el-Kebir, after which he was obdurate in his refusal to negotiate further. Cunningham helped to overcome this by sending the captains of his cruisers and destroyers to talk to the captains of the French cruisers and destroyers, and persuade them that the honourable course was to fall in with the British proposals. This was successful in that Godfroy was supported by his captains in his later acceptance of the terms. The French demilitarised their ships by landing the guns' breech blocks, discharging oil fuel and reducing to a skeleton complement. They remained in Alexandria for the next three years. Cunningham's cool head and adroit exploitation of the existing trust and friendship with Godfroy resulted in a peaceful solution. When one compares the events at Alexandria and Oran, it is evident that the personalities of the principal contenders played a part. Cunningham was a formidable operator who carried considerable clout. He was ready to turn a blind eye to some of Churchill's more dictatorial instructions, and did so; and the negotiations were prolonged beyond the time-scale set by the Government. Somerville on the other hand did not carry such authority, nor had he had any earlier opportunity to establish personal rapport with Gensoul. Moreover the latter, in contrast to Godfroy in Alexandria, was completely loyal to the Pétain Government.

Force H's start could hardly have been more dramatic. Within a few days of the force being formed, Britain's battleships had been in action for the first time in the war, but their target had been not the enemy German Fleet, but that of its French ally of three weeks before. There was much anguish in the higher levels of command about the action, but Churchill's firmness of direction allowed no opposition, and dissenting voices became marked men: their views were noted and were sometimes held against them when consideration was later given to their fitness to command. Both North and Somerville were to feel the effect of this.

NAVAL ENTERPRISE AND POLITICAL CONFUSION

OPERATING IN THE MEDITERRANEAN: CLUB RUNS

IN **JULY 1940**, when Britain was down but not out after Dunkirk and Oran, and when only the opening shots of the Battle of Britain had been fired, Churchill took the bold decision to reinforce the Middle East. As a result the Mediterranean remained, for the next two years, a shifting scene reflecting the campaigns being fought in that theatre, and this in turn influenced Britain's maritime strategy.

The direct line of communications to Britain's Army of the Nile in Egypt ran through the Mediterranean. Italy was in a dominant position to strangle that supply route. The main threat came from the air, as the airfields in Sardinia and Sicily were ideally sited to control the passage from Gibraltar to Malta. For the last 400 miles, or twenty-eight hours for a 14-knot convoy, ships would be within 150 miles of those airfields and be open to high-level dive-bombing and torpedo-bombing attacks. Savoia SM 79 bombers and torpedo bombers, CR 42 Fiat biplane fighters and Cant 506B reconnaissance floatplanes were the main aircraft used by the Italian Air Force in its actions against Force H. The Luftwaffe had not yet been deployed to the area.

Italy possessed a formidable navy. There were the two new battleships, *Littorio* and *Vittorio Veneto*, of 35,000 tons carrying 15-inch guns, and five older Cavour class with 12.6-inch guns, of which *Giulio Cesare* and *Comte di Cavour* had been modernised. Together with seven heavy cruisers, Zara class with 8-inch guns, and other 6-inch-gun cruisers, they formed the main units of the Fleet. There were no aircraft carriers. In June 1940 the Fleet was spread around several bases. In the western Mediterranean these were Naples (with *Littorio*, four light cruisers, fourteen torpedo boats carrying four torpedoes each, and eleven submarines), Spezia (one battleship, twelve escort destroyers, eighteen submarines), Messina and Augusta in Sicily (four heavy cruisers, three light cruisers, sixteen fleet destroyers, eight MTBs or motor torpedo boats), and Cagliari in Sardinia (eight destroyers, eighteen submarines). And in the eastern Mediterranean, at the main naval base of Taranto, there were three battleships, three heavy cruisers, five light cruisers, twenty fleet destroyers, eight escort destroyers and twenty-two submarines. There was a mining threat east of the Skerki Bank in the shallower waters south of Sicily known as the Narrows; there was also a threat here from the E-boats based at Pantellaria.

Although Italy's Navy greatly exceeded British naval strength in the Mediterranean, her naval strategy was essentially defensive, a failing which contributed to the overrunning of her army in North Africa through lack of control of sea communications. The Italians did not understand the importance of eliminating Malta, which was as much an air base as it was a naval base, nor of accepting battle offered by the Royal Navy on numerous occasions. Initially it was anticipated that the considerable Italian submarine strength would prove a severe threat. Yet the Italian U-boats achieved very little and did not become the major factor in the control of the sea routes, as experienced in the Atlantic. They suffered heavy losses and the numbers on patrol were soon reduced to ten at each end of the Mediterranean.

Before Italy's entry into the war she had had an arrangement with Germany that each country's navy would retain full liberty of action in its own theatre, but that intelligence and technical developments would be exchanged. The German Navy would be responsible for submarine and surface-vessel operations in the Atlantic, and would keep the two battlecruisers *Scharnhorst* and *Gneisenau* in the North Sea in order to force the French and British to station the greatest number of capital ships outside the Mediterranean. The

Italian Navy would play a part in the submarine war in the Atlantic south of Lisbon, and possibly send surface vessels and submarines into the Indian Ocean. In the Mediterranean it would 'seek to bring to action the greatest number of enemy forces'.[1]

Britain's naval strength in the Mediterranean was divided, as we have seen. In the eastern basin the Mediterranean Fleet at Alexandria was reinforced and now comprised four battleships, one carrier, six cruisers, sixteen destroyers, three sloops and ten submarines. In March 1940, in anticipation of Italy's entry into the war, a French squadron of a battleship, four cruisers and three destroyers was sent to Alexandria to operate under the Commander-in-Chief of the Mediterranean Fleet, Admiral Sir Andrew Cunningham. In the western basin Force H now assumed responsibility. There was continual co-operation between the two Commanders. When an operation was being carried out at one end of the Mediterranean, the other would try to provide a diversion at his end.

Between these two separate forces lay Malta. Before the war the island had been considered indefensible against Italian air power and its defences had been long neglected. It now relied on supplies coming from both ends of the Mediterranean, and these were to become major fleet operations. The passage to Malta and onwards to the eastern Mediterranean was considered too dangerous for troop and other convoys, which had to proceed round South Africa and the Cape of Good Hope, a six-week voyage of over 12,500 miles. There were some exceptions, and a few heavily escorted merchant ships with stores for Malta and the Army of the Nile made the hazardous passage.

It was in this setting and against these enemy forces that Force H would operate in the Mediterranean for the rest of 1940. On return from the second attack by Force H on *Dunkerque* at Mers-el-Kebir, preparations were made to carry out an air strike on the French battleship *Richelieu* at Dakar, but this operation was transferred to a Home Fleet squadron under the command of *Hermes*. Instead the force was required to provide a diversion for a convoy in the eastern Mediterranean sailing from Alexandria to Malta. *Hood, Valiant, Resolution* and *Ark Royal*, with three cruisers and ten destroyers, sailed from Gibraltar on 8 July to carry out an air attack on Cagliari. The force was heavily attacked by Italian Savoia aircraft the following afternoon and evening. Radar reports from *Valiant* gave some notice of the strike but an attack down-sun came without warning. Some forty aircraft took part, dropping about a hundred bombs, released from 10,000–13,000 feet in patterns using stick bombing. The attacks were pressed home, and although no hits were obtained the bombing accuracy compared favourably with German attacks. This was

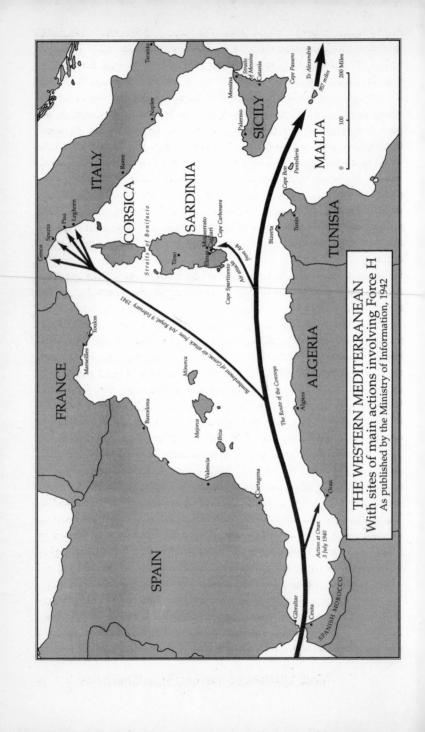

THE WESTERN MEDITERRANEAN
With sites of main actions involving Force H
As published by the Ministry of Information, 1942

Force H's first contact with the Italian Air Force, and Somerville concluded that there was little chance of *Ark Royal* escaping damage while operating within 100 miles of the Sardinian coast, as had been planned for the next morning. In his view the risk of the ship being put out of action, with the loss of a large number of aircraft, for a minor operation intended only to act as a diversion was not justified, and he withdrew the force to the west. During the night *Forester* sighted a submarine at short range on the surface and attempted to ram. The submarine crash-dived and fired a torpedo from her stern tube which hit *Escort. Forester* later obtained a firm contact and attacked with depth charges, but to no visible result. It proved too difficult to tow *Escort* as her rudder was jammed, and although an attempt was made to tow her stern first, she sank later that morning. A prolonged search for the submarine by destroyers was hampered by poor sonar conditions, which gave submarines complete cover and made day hunting abortive. On 23 July *Ark Royal* escorted by one cruiser and four destroyers sailed to carry out attacks on merchant shipping in Le Verdun Roads and at Bordeaux, but the Admiralty cancelled the operation two days later, the first of many last-minute changes that were to bedevil the force.

Because Force H had been so hastily assembled, Somerville now planned to carry out a programme of exercises and practices with the object of welding a varied collection of ships into a homogeneous fighting unit. In particular the gunnery and anti-submarine efficiency left a lot to be desired; the destroyers had become too much convoy-orientated and needed more fleet work. Unfortunately the departure of five destroyers of the 13th Destroyer Flotilla to the UK allowed only individual practices to be carried out by cruisers and destroyers; these included full-calibre and sub-calibre firings east of the Rock. Ships in harbour were given daily communication, height-finding and other air-defence exercises. The frequent presence over the Rock of unidentified reconnaissance aircraft and two air raids during this period gave an added spur to the exercises. As already noted, the Gibraltar defences, much criticised by Somerville, were also improved. Somerville argued, moreover, that unless air reconnaissance was available to a sufficient depth to both the east and west of Gibraltar, the risk of enemy vessels breaking in or out of the Straits was greatly increased during conditions of low visibility; and he supported a request from 200 Group RAF for a permanent deployment of two Sunderlands.

The long-deferred reinforcement of the air defences and the military garrison of Malta was at last begun. Somerville was told that a transport was being sent to Gibraltar carrying Hurricanes for Malta. He at once suggested that instead of submitting such a valuable cargo to that dangerous passage the aircraft should be assembled at Gibraltar, placed on board *Ark Royal* and flown off to Malta from a position within the limit of their endurance.[2] This suggestion was approved, but with the old carrier *Argus* being used instead of *Ark Royal*.

On 31 July the force sailed on the first of what were to become known as Club Runs – the flying off of RAF fighters for Malta and/or the passage of ships through to the eastern Mediterranean. On this occasion, *Argus* was to fly off twelve Hurricanes with two Skuas as escort. The force was attacked next day by aircraft and about eighty bombs dropped. In the afternoon eight aircraft in three sub-flights approached from the port beam at 12,000 feet. Gunfire from the fleet was effective and two aircraft turned away before bomb release. A second wave of nine aircraft attacked a few minutes later on the port quarter and an emergency turn in that direction was made to bring the attack on to the beam so that all guns could bear. Again, several aircraft sheered off before releasing their bombs. The attacks were not pressed home with the same determination as in the previous operation, and this was attributed to the marked improvement in AA gunfire. In the evening the force split into two groups: Group 1, consisting of *Hood, Ark Royal, Enterprise* and three destroyers, was to carry out air attacks on Elmas air station at Cagliari; and Group 2 – *Valiant, Resolution, Argus*, one cruiser and seven destroyers – was to continue eastward to fly off the Hurricanes at dawn. The cruiser *Enterprise* was detached to transmit confusing radio signals. The air strike obtained direct hits on four hangars and other aerodrome buildings, and four aircraft in the open were destroyed. One Swordfish crashed on taking off from *Ark Royal* and another made a forced landing in Sardinia. Group 2 flew off the Hurricanes in two flights. Two Sunderlands flying from Gibraltar to provide additional escort did not make contact. All Hurricanes and escorting Skuas arrived safely and the Admiralty sent their congratulations on the success of this first and novel supply operation.

Somerville confided his feelings during the operation in a letter to his wife:[3]

Everyone seems pleased with the results of the operation and if we hadn't lost the crew of one aircraft we should have got away with a clean sheet. I think we must have shaken those ice creamers a bit. About 2.30am in the pitch dark on Friday morning as we were mucking about only 100 miles or so off the Iti coast I thought of all the possibilities – destroyers, MTBs, submarines, cruisers, bombing attacks at daylight, etc., and began to feel that it was all a bit sticky and the temperature of my feet dropped appreciably. And then in the pitch dark I saw a small shadow separate itself from the great shadow of the *Ark*. The first Swordfish taking off. And then I thought of those incredibly gallant chaps taking off in the pitch dark to fly 140 miles to a place they've never seen, to be shot up by AA guns and dazzled by searchlights and then mark you to fly over the sea and find that tiny floating aerodrome with the knowledge if they don't find it they're done. Well that shook me up and I realised how small were my personal difficulties compared to theirs. The wind changed completely while they were away and some only just got back. It was an anxious time waiting for them but a heartening moment when they came trundling back one after the other under the low clouds.

The Club Runs became fairly standard events in that they were confined to one general route along the North African coast and one particular destination, Malta. The general form was that the fighters, Hurricanes in the early days, arrived in Gibraltar either in the carrier they were to be flown off from or, more often, in crates. They would then be assembled and embarked in *Ark Royal*. The flying-off position would be south-west of Sardinia, about 400–500 miles from Malta. In the earlier trips Skuas or Fulmars acted as escort. If the escort was to be provided by planes from Gibraltar, generally Glenn Martins or Blenheims or Hudsons, the normal practice was that they rendezvoused with the fleet and circled the carrier until its flight had flown off and formed up, when they would head off for Malta. In good flying conditions the Hurricanes generally became airborne along the flight deck about halfway between the bridge structure and the bows of *Ark Royal*; very occasionally there was a near-bellyflop. If bad weather at Gibraltar prevented escorting aircraft from taking off, the force would remain at sea in the vicinity. Between August 1940 and October 1942, no fewer than 764 aircraft were flown through to Malta from a number of carriers in this way, Hurricanes until March 1942 and Spitfires thereafter. Of these, twelve returned to land on their carrier, no mean feat especially with no arrestor hook fitted and carried out by pilots with no deck-landing experience. Thirty-four planes were lost in flight. This was not the only way of reinforcing the Middle East. Another route was to ship the fighters in crates to Takoradi on the Gold Coast. There they would be assembled and flown across Africa to Egypt. The *Argus* was the first to make this trip in September1940, carrying thirty Hurricanes.

On return to Gibraltar *Hood, Valiant* and *Argus* sailed back to Britain. Somerville transferred his flag to *Renown* at Scapa Flow and, with his senior staff officers, visited the Admiralty for talks. Besides matters of immediate concern in forthcoming operations, he learnt of Admiralty policy in other the-atres that could affect Force H. In the event of a Japanese attack on Malaysia, *Renown* and *Ark Royal* would probably be sent to Colombo in Ceylon to pro-tect trade routes, together with a reinforcement of cruisers and destroyers. If Japan attacked Australasia the Mediterranean Fleet might be sent to the Far East and a squadron of R class battleships be stationed at Gibraltar to confine the Italian Fleet to the Mediterranean; *Renown* and *Ark Royal* might still be sent to the East Indies Station. There were plans for offensive action against Spanish ports and forces in the event of Spanish intervention, and proposals for mining Spanish ports; and, if Spain should enter the war, of occupying the Cape Verde Islands to deny them to the enemy.

Renown sailed from Scapa for Gibraltar on 10 August, having to divert for a short period to patrol off Iceland when it appeared possible that a German force was about to sail from Norway. *Ark Royal, Enterprise* and six destroyers from Gibraltar rendezvoused on the return passage and the force carried out flying practices and exercises. By this time Admiral Wells had struck his flag in *Ark Royal* and the not altogether happy arrangement of having two vice admirals in Force H was brought to an end. At Gibraltar there were three air raids during the night of 20/21 August. One aircraft was shot down by a salvo from *Renown*; subsequent recovery of the wing proved it to be an Italian plane. The force sailed again for further exercises in the Atlantic, joining up for the last two days of the passage to Gibraltar of reinforcements for the Mediterranean Fleet, which was to be the purpose of the next operation. At this time there was also an urgent requirement for an armoured brigade to reach Egypt before the big land battle expected to start shortly. But the pas-sage of the ships carrying Mechanical Transport (MT ships) would, it was considered, hazard the success of the whole operation and those were sent round the Cape.

Force H and the Mediterranean Fleet reinforcements sailed from Gibraltar on 30 August. The force consisted of *Renown*, the battleship *Valiant*, the carriers *Illustrious, Ark Royal*, three cruisers and seventeen destroyers. The operation marked a notable event in the development of air defence of the fleet. For the first time there were two modern carriers working together with four radar-fitted ships in company. Each carrier acted as fighter-directing ship for its own fighters, *Illustrious* being free to use her radar as occasion demanded. The remaining radar-fitted ships guarded sectors: *Sheffield* to the eastward, *Coventry* to the westward and *Valiant* all round. The organisation worked well and gave the fleet a feeling of confidence; surprise attack without radar warning was most unlikely. The use of W/T for passing reports allowed fighters to be directed on to shadowers with minimum delay. Next morning, 31 August, although no risks from mines were expected, paravanes were streamed before the fleet became liable to heavy air attack. In the evening two destroyers, *Velox* and *Wishart*, were detached to make a diversion north of the Balearic Islands. They were to transmit messages by W/T designed to mislead the enemy into thinking that during the night the whole force had maintained its north-easterly course towards the Gulf of Genoa.

The following day, 1 September, nine Swordfish from *Ark Royal* carried out a night attack on Elmas airfield at Cagliari, adding to the damage from the previous raid on 2 August. All aircraft returned safely. Two fighter patrols, each of six aircraft, were maintained over the fleet throughout the day and two shadowing aircraft were shot down. In the evening *Illustrious*, *Valiant*, two cruisers and eight destroyers parted company north-east of Skerki Bank to proceed to Malta. Force H steered west to reach a suitable position for a second strike on Cagliari during the night. Nine Swordfish attacked the aerodrome and power station. They met heavy but erratic AA barrage fire, but once again all aircraft got back to base safely. The force returned to Gibraltar on 3 September. During the operation it was within effective bombing range from Italian air bases for forty-eight hours. Heavy air attack had been expected, even hoped for, in anticipation of inflicting a telling blow on the Italian Air Force from the strong concentration of AA fire and number of fighter patrols available to the force. The lack of surface and air opposition was attributed to the successful Balearic diversion, the destruction of shadowers by day and the first attack on the aerodrome. Five destroyers escorting the reinforcements to Malta arrived back in Gibraltar on 5 September.

OPERATING IN THE ATLANTIC

In the early months of the war the Germans deployed converted merchant ships as raiders in the central Atlantic, supported by tankers and supply ships. By the end of the year fifty-four merchantmen had been lost. Important convoys had to be escorted. The first of the Middle East convoys, labelled WS convoys and known as 'Winston's Specials', sailed at the end of June. Consisting of up to twenty-five ships sailing about monthly, each escorted by a cruiser or capital ship, they were to become a regular feature, and 150 of the Allies' best merchant ships were permanently employed for this service. From August to December 1940 the troopships carried 76,000 men from the UK. Their routes varied but the general pattern was to proceed west from the Clyde into the Atlantic, some passing west of the Azores, to Freetown in Sierra Leone. Freetown became an important staging post for convoys. It was not a satisfactory convoy assembly port or command location, but once Dakar and the co-operation of French warships were denied after the fall of France its deficiencies had to be accepted. The convoys called there to replenish fuel, water and stores. Up to two HG convoys (Homeward bound from Gibraltar) were also sailed each month. The latter were under the control of the Flag Officer Commanding the North Atlantic Station and were escorted by local forces, which included the 13th Destroyer Flotilla. Force H destroyers could also provide escort if required and available. Later the force was to find itself escorting slow SL convoys from Freetown. The safety of the Atlantic islands had also acquired greater strategic importance. Because of their central location the Azores were in a dominating position, and if occupied by the Germans could threaten these routes. Force H was the nearest available British force to defend against any German attempt to take over the islands.

Force H had now been in existence for two months. Somerville had conducted two operations in the Mediterranean, in addition to the original Oran expedition, and the force had been exercised in its operational role. But French matters again intervened and a major part of the squadron had to be relinquished temporarily for an attack on Dakar. This was to involve Somerville in controversy.

Attack on Dakar

The safety of the shipping route to Freetown would be threatened if the French colony of Senegal, with its base at Dakar, came under German control. General de Gaulle proposed to establish his Free French movement in the colony, a move welcomed by Churchill who initiated the operation, code-named Menace. At short notice a force was put together in the UK of 4200 British and 2700 Free French troops, and on 31 August it sailed from the Clyde for Freetown. The naval force, called Force M, was commanded by Vice Admiral J. H. D. Cunningham and in due course consisted of two battleships, one carrier, five cruisers and ten destroyers. The cruiser *Fiji* was torpedoed on passage and took no further part. *Resolution, Barham, Ark Royal* and eight destroyers were detached from Force H to join Force M. Somerville, although experienced at Oran and supplying the bulk of the naval force, was not put in charge of the operation; the First Sea Lord explained to him that its Commander needed to be in close touch with de Gaulle and the British Government.[4]

While Force M was on passage to Freetown a Vichy French force of three cruisers and three destroyers were allowed to pass through the Straits of Gibraltar unopposed on 11 September, presenting a clear threat to the Dakar expedition. Although it was too late to intercept them, the Admiralty ordered Force H, now consisting only of *Renown* and three destroyers, to sea to contact the French ships and tell them they could proceed to Casablanca but not to Dakar or the Biscay ports. Minimum force was to be used to enforce these instructions. Somerville kept to the southward with a view to staying ahead of the French force should it continue past Casablanca. A close inshore patrol could not be established as the French had made it clear they would open fire on any ships or aircraft within 20 miles of the coast. The French ships were not sighted and the force returned to Gibraltar. After two nights in harbour it was off again on 17 September to patrol south of Casablanca but was later redirected to patrol south-west of the Straits ready to intercept any French forces located by patrols in the Straits themselves. It was subsequently decided there would be a better chance of interception if *Renown* was stationed at Gibraltar and the patrols were carried out to the eastward.

After much signalling and complaints from Somerville about being given too little information, not least about the Dakar operation and the difficulty of deciding whether avoidance of incidents should take priority over control of movements of French warships, the Admiralty did issue some guidance about their interception and that of French merchant shipping (see p. 52 below). Even so, Somerville had no news that the Dakar attack had started until he heard it on a BBC broadcast. His anger at the way in which the whole affair was being pursued is evident in his letters to his wife:[5] 'It's all a proper ghastly muddle and we simply don't know where we are or whom we are supposed to be fighting.' The Dakar adventure, just like Oran, was too precipitate and a political blunder: 'given more time we should probably have got what we wanted'. And 'if the French continue to attack us at Gibraltar it will be quite impossible for me to control the western Mediterranean'. All in all 'it simply maddens me we could have been so stupid'. After two days of fruitless patrolling he intended to return to Gibraltar but delayed his return for twenty-four hours on receiving a report that Pierre Laval, Pétain's pro-Nazi deputy, had asked Germany to release the whole Toulon fleet to attack him; nothing further was heard.

As a result of security leaks all surprise for the operation had been lost. In one incident at Liverpool the evening before the ships sailed, a Frenchman at a dinner in the Adelphi Hotel had publicly proposed the toast 'à la Dakar'. When additional French cruisers arrived at Dakar from Casablanca the British Government concluded that the operation had become impracticable. But de Gaulle was adamant that they should persevere, and Cunningham with his Army colleague were given authority 'to do what they thought best to give effect to the original purpose of the expedition'.[6] They decided that they would go ahead on 23 September. Mist and poor visibility that morning made air reconnaissance and spotting for ships' gunfire tricky; the attempt to win over the airfield failed; and de Gaulle's emissaries to the Vichy Governor were rebuffed. The opening shots of the action came from French forts firing at the British destroyers, and the whole fleet was soon under fire. When *Forester* was straddled by three 15-inch shells from *Richelieu*, the dye in the huge columns of water turned the ensign at the foremast head yellow. The Government's directive that the operation should be carried out if at all possible without bloodshed allowed only a few salvoes to be fired at the forts in return. A message was received from the French confirming that all landings would be opposed.

It was decided to go ahead with the original plan to make a peaceful landing 10 miles east of the town. But communications between Cunningham and de Gaulle broke down and the transport with the Free French troops could not be found in the now dense fog. The main landing had to be cancelled. A minor landing in the evening by the Free French troops on the opposite side of the bay was repulsed. After a day of failure and confusion, and with the Allied forces in an unfavourable and dangerous state lying off a hostile coast in thick fog, an ultimatum was given to the Vichy authorities demanding acceptance of the Allied terms by 0600 the next day. The reply was an unqualified refusal.

At dawn on 24 September the British Fleet engaged the French warships in harbour and *Ark Royal's* aircraft attacked *Richelieu*. The targets became obscured by smoke and the British disengaged, but they resumed the bombardment in the afternoon. Neither the *Richelieu* nor the shore batteries were put out of action and the duel petered out in the afternoon. *Barham* received four hits. Cunningham consulted with de Gaulle. It was decided to land British troops the following day and renew the bombardment in a bid to secure the final destruction of the French warships. Next morning *Resolution* was torpedoed by a Vichy submarine and seriously damaged. The gunfire duel was resumed; while the French fire was accurate, British fire had doubtful effect. It was now evident that Dakar was unlikely to surrender and that the Royal Navy ships would suffer more damage before the French ships were put out of action. The force withdrew, without landing any British troops. This first attempt at an amphibious operation had ended in total failure.[7] The cost to the Navy was one battleship out of action for a year, two cruisers damaged and nine aircraft destroyed.

The day after the attack French planes carried out a heavy retaliatory raid on Gibraltar. In the afternoon a number of Vichy bombers took advantage of the cover given by a high Levanter cloud and bombed for more than two hours. *Renown* left harbour with all her AA guns firing. Of the 150 bombs dropped, seventy-five appeared to have been deliberately jettisoned in the bay. There was another raid the following day lasting three hours, heavier than the day before but with two-thirds of the bombs again being jettisoned over the water. One anti-submarine trawler alongside the south mole was sunk. There was some damage ashore and Admiral North's secretary was killed. At one period Gibraltar wireless was off the air. Vichy admitted to the loss of twelve bombers.

When Somerville finally returned to Gibraltar on 7 October he was shocked to learn that the Admiralty had instructed North, commanding the North Atlantic Station, to report why he had not ordered *Renown* to sea when the French squadron of three cruisers and three destroyers passed through the Straits on 11 September. These ships had sailed from Toulon on 9 September. The signalled information of their departure, originally supplied by the Naval Attaché Madrid but with their destination unstated, was received in London just before midnight on 10 September, and the ships passed Gibraltar at 0845 next morning. Somerville submitted to the Admiralty that he had acted in the belief that the decision was his alone, and if the action taken was considered to have been incorrect he wished to accept full responsibility.[8] He had brought Force H to one hour's notice after he was sent a sighting report from *Hotspur*, but had reverted to normal notice on receiving no orders to intercept; there was no reason to assume that the Admiralty was unaware of the movement of the French ships as the departure signal had been relayed to Gibraltar from London. He and North had fully discussed the situation and both were of the opinion that the Government did not want them to interfere with the movement of the ships. Their orders at the time were to avoid incidents with the French. The initial Admiralty policy for dealing with French warships attempting to pass through the Straits, issued on 4 July after the attack on Oran, had been that ships were to be prepared to attack but were not to fire the first shot; and that contact with equal or superior French forces should be avoided. The Admiralty had also warned 'that the attack on Dakar may lead the Vichy government to declare war on us and attack Gibraltar by air'.[9] And on 12 July the Admiralty had signalled that no further action was to be taken against French ships in their colonial and North African ports, but reserved the right to deal with warships proceeding to the enemy-controlled Bay of Biscay ports.

Bearing in mind also that the orders for the Dakar operation required that it be carried out without bloodshed if at all possible, North had concluded, Somerville concurring, that in the absence of orders from home the French ships transiting the Straits on 11 September were free to make the passage to Casablanca or Dakar, and that his duty lay solely in keeping the Admiralty informed of any such movements. He had reported *Hotspur*'s sighting at 0617, and an hour later signalled that he intended to keep an eye on the force by air and would report its probable destination. The Admiralty had had ample time to order *Renown* to sea if it had desired. The ship had been brought to one hour's notice and could have sailed at 0715. As already noted, the Admiralty had received the initial intelligence signal about the ships during the night of 10/11 September, but the Director of Operations (Foreign) did not show it to the First Sea Lord, Admiral of the Fleet Sir Dudley Pound, until the following morning, too late for the latter to have ordered *Renown* to sea to intercept.

Subsequently Pound took the view that, although Force H was constituted as a detached squadron under Somerville's command, no mention was made of it being an independent command. Although the Admiralty generally controlled its movements there was no reason why North could not do so in an emergency; thus he could have ordered *Renown* to sea and then have informed the Admiralty. Pound decided that North no longer retained his confidence and, with the agreement of the First Lord, A. V. Alexander, relieved him of his command.[10]

North was allowed to represent his case, but was denied any formal inquiry. His censure and sacking caused wide resentment in the Navy, with other admirals including Sir Andrew Cunningham protesting against his treatment. Churchill had once before suggested that North should be relieved, after he was critical about the action at Oran, and this coupled with the humiliation over the débâcle at Dakar paved the way for his dismissal. A biography of Sir Dudley Pound published in 2000 makes the point that it was North's lack of action which lost him the First Sea Lord's confidence and suggests that the latter was wrong to try and give reasons for relieving him; to a certain extent the French ships were irrelevant. North was left in no doubt of Pound's attitude towards him.[11]

The circumstances alone did not justify North's removal from his command. But if the High Command loses confidence in a commander then, especially in wartime, replacement is likely to be the consequence. Somerville remained loyal to North, as his letters show. Despite campaigns on his behalf, it was not until after the war that North's name was cleared, and that was after Churchill's retirement from politics. The episode has been given thorough analysis by Arthur Marder in his book *Operation Menace: The Dakar Expedition and the Dudley North Affair*. This distinguished naval historian gave his opinion that the statement made by Prime Minister Harold Macmillan to the House of Commons in May 1957, which was decided upon after he had conferred with five Admirals of the Fleet, was 'Solomon–like in its wisdom, restoring North's honour while at the same time not unduly denigrating the Admiralty'.[12] It was nonetheless inexcusable that it took seventeen years to settle the matter.

The Admiralty, having held North as the Senior Officer to blame for not ordering *Renown* to sea, exonerated Somerville on the ground that he did not receive sufficient warning in time to take action to intercept the ships. Somerville riposted that, even if he had received sufficient notice to enable *Renown* and one or two destroyers to proceed to sea, he would have refrained from doing so for reasons he had already reported, namely that there was insufficient destroyer escort and it was unlikely he could make sufficient ground to the westward to avoid being sighted by the French force. He considered that Casablanca was the probable destination and that it was unlikely that the force would proceed to a Bay of Biscay port. To his wife he wrote, 'He [North] and I are both furious about it and the dirty trick of making us naval officers responsible for a damn bad political blunder.'[13] As a result of this unhappy affair, revised terms of reference for Force H were issued (see p. 13 above).

At the end of September 1940 *Renown* and four destroyers sailed to intercept *Richelieu*, which was reported to be proceeding from Dakar to a Bay of Biscay port. But the Admiralty diverted the force to the Azores after a report that two German merchant ships with troops onboard had been seen in the Bay of Biscay; it was possible their mission might be to capture the Azores. Nothing materialised, but Somerville was told to continue the watch on the Atlantic islands, and two British transports on their way home from the abortive Dakar expedition were held in readiness to land troops on the Azores. On 12 October the Admiralty ordered *Renown*, then at twelve hours' notice carrying out repairs, and attendant destroyers to be clear of Gibraltar to the westward in anticipation of possible French reprisals on Gibraltar in the wake of forth-coming Allied operations in Syria. The destroyers were later detailed to hunt a submarine which had shelled a ship in the area. The submarine was not detected and the damaged ship, still afloat, had to be sunk as being a danger to navigation.

The French battlecruiser *Strasbourg*, which had escaped from Oran, now briefly re-entered the scene. On 17 October it was reported that she and twenty units of the French Fleet were preparing to leave Toulon. The Admiralty ordered a homeward-bound convoy escorted by the cruiser *Australia* to return to Gibraltar and Force H destroyers to establish a patrol to the eastward. No French movement resulted but the patrolling destroyers were able to carry out anti-submarine sweeps which led to an attack on an Italian U-boat by *Firedrake* and *Wrestler*. The submarine surfaced and was boarded before sinking. Code books and papers recovered showed that another submarine was operating south of Alborán, an island 100 miles east of Gibraltar. Six destroyers were despatched to hunt it down, and this submarine was also sunk. These attacks were carried out by ships of the 13th and 8th Destroyer Flotillas. Four ships of the latter returned to Gibraltar from the Dakar operation the next day, 19 October. After that operation they had been employed escorting WS convoys, sailing as far south as 10 degrees South; *Forester* had taken de Gaulle to Douala in the Cameroons. On 27 October *Sheffield* sailed to patrol off the Azores with the object of intercepting German troop movements from Biscay ports should the enemy attempt to occupy the islands.

The Admiralty's policy for dealing with French ship movements through the Straits continued to change. At the end of September the policy was that escorted French merchant ships were not to be interfered with. But as the ships stayed in Spanish territorial waters as much as possible and were nearly always escorted, this meant that there was no effective control, and it was not until November that an interception was made. In October a new policy, called Ration, to prevent the French making a hole in the blockade, required that convoyed ships be taken to Gibraltar but escorts be allowed to proceed. Somerville pointed out that interception of convoys necessarily involved entry into Spanish and French territorial waters.[14] While the former had to be respected, experience showed that intrusion into the latter would be likely to bring French retaliation on Gibraltar. It was not clear to him how the policy of infringing territorial waters to enforce the blockade could be reconciled with the contrary policy adopted in relation with other neutral countries. Unless Spanish territorial waters were infringed, no interception to the eastward could be carried out nearer than 155 miles from Gibraltar. In the Atlantic merchant ships if unescorted were to be sent to Freetown for examination. But, again, as most were escorted there was no effective control of contraband traffic. Somerville continued to point out that interception of merchant shipping under Ration not only imposed a heavy strain on destroyers but limited very severely the activity of A/S (anti-submarine) patrols in the local area and of training practices of ships and aircraft. These commitments also ruled out establishing a standing patrol to the east or west at a distance that would enable it to give sufficient warning to Force H ships that they should leave harbour and intercept approaching high-speed war vessels. It was decided that an extended surface patrol should only be established when there was good reason to believe that a 'break in or out' of the Mediterranean was probable.[15]

Somerville was concerned that the full support of Force H should be available in case attempts were made by superior French surface or air forces to release a captured convoy before it reached Gibraltar. A confrontation in such a confined area as the Straits was neither seamanlike nor desirable; if there had to be a fight, it should be conducted at sea. When *Renown* carried out an interception operation, Somerville's general instructions to destroyers in company were that, if French warships passed westwards through the Straits, confirmation should be obtained that they would not proceed beyond Casablanca. Destroyers should steer to intercept. When interception was assured, destroyers should concentrate. If the order to stop was not obeyed, *Renown* was to fire rounds ahead of the ships to enforce compliance. If this was not successful, the French ships were to be engaged. Ships could approach within 20 miles of the Vichy French coast if necessary. If *Strasbourg* should pass through the Straits she should be shadowed, whether going north or south, and prevented, after due warning, from going north. If one or more cruisers or four or more destroyers passed through, they were to be shadowed and prevented from moving north only.[16] In October the policy stipulated that warships were not allowed to proceed to ports south of Dakar, and that all submarines except those on the surface and under escort should be treated as hostile.[17]

At the end of October there was a possibility that French capital ships would pass through the Straits: *Strasbourg* from Toulon, *Jean Bart* from Casablanca and *Richelieu* from Dakar. In Force H's absence from Gibraltar, submarine patrols were set up to prevent the passage of the latter two ships; if possible they were to be warned by a surface vessel to return to Casablanca, but as a last resort they might be torpedoed without warning. As all his ships would be away at the time, Somerville noted drily that the battleships would be given the warning by a trawler or armed yacht patrolling off Tangier.

On 31 October the Consul-General Tangier reported a rumour that French ships at Casablanca might sail at any moment. On receiving a sighting report of five French destroyers in the Mediterranean on a westerly course, *Renown*, *Barham* and four destroyers sailed. It turned out, however, that the destroyers were making for Casablanca, and no outward movement from that port was revealed. Force H returned to harbour after carrying out long-range full-calibre 15-inch throw-off firings by *Renown* and *Barham*, and 4.7-inch throw-off firings by the destroyers. Further preparations for French ship movements were overturned by a report that the German pocket battleship *Admiral Scheer* was operating in the north Atlantic. On 6 November the

Admiralty ordered *Renown* and a destroyer screen to proceed with despatch into the Atlantic. Not knowing for how long this would be, Somerville transferred his whole staff and office. The signal was received in the middle of the night at 0130 and the ship sailed at 0300 after disembarking the complete organisation. His flag was transferred to *Ark Royal* later that day on her return from the UK, where she had had a short refit after the Dakar expedition. *Sheffield* also returned from her Azores patrol and together with the rejoined destroyers would have brought Force H up to full strength again, except that the flagship *Renown* had now been detached. Somerville was glad to have *Ark Royal* back; without her, he said, he was 'like a blind man without a dog'.

BACK IN THE MEDITERRANEAN

With *Ark Royal* the flagship, Force H sailed next day, 7 November 1940, for a succession of operations in the Mediterranean. Following the Italian invasion of Greece in October, there was heightened tension in the eastern Mediterranean. Force H's task was to cover reinforcements to the Mediterranean Fleet and to fly off Hurricanes for Malta. In the first operation the reinforcements consisted of *Barham*, two cruisers *Glasgow* and *Berwick* and three destroyers, carrying between them 2150 troops for Malta, and escorted by *Ark Royal*, *Sheffield* and eight destroyers. Three of the Force H destroyers were also to accompany the reinforcements through to Malta. Strict security measures were imposed on the passage of the troops. None were to appear on deck dressed in khaki until the ships were 6 miles clear of Europa Point; soldiers wearing naval overalls might go on deck but they were not to wear military caps. These precautions were necessary because there were numerous fishing boats in the Straits and it was assumed they were paid to report movements to the enemy. The forecast fine weather made it likely that the force would be detected and attacked by bombers. Somerville therefore went on ahead with *Ark Royal*, *Glasgow*, *Sheffield* and six destroyers to carry out an air strike on Cagliari early on the morning of 9 November before the force was attacked. A shadowing Savoia SM 79 was shot down. Nine Swordfish bombed the aerodrome, registering hits on buildings, hangars, seaplanes and AA batteries. There was little opposition and no British casualties. Three Fulmars for *Illustrious* were also flown off and arrived safely at Malta. The striking force rejoined and the whole force was formed up before the first air attack, which came later that morning.

Radar detected a shadower at 29 miles that proved to be a Cant floatplane; it was shot down by a Fulmar. Radar also revealed a large formation 50 miles ahead of the fleet. This allowed interception by Fulmars and Skuas, but although they obtained hits on the enemy they did not break the formation. The enemy attack, from 13,000 feet, in one big wave of four sections each of five bombers, launched a continuous stick of bombs dropped across the fleet, which was formed in two columns disposed abeam. *Barham* and *Ark Royal* were straddled and had near-misses, but there was no damage or casualties in any ship. Later that day the reinforcements continued on their way to Malta according to plan, and Force H made an uneventful return passage to Gibraltar. Wind conditions allowed intensive flying and control exercises and, in particular, enabled new pilots to practise deck landing.

The optimism about dealing with air attacks expressed at the time of the previous attack by Italian aircraft on 31 July was tempered after this operation. The AA fire was disappointing, consistently bursting short, and the fighters were unable to break up the enemy formation. Effective attacks on Savoias were handicapped by the small margin of speed enjoyed by the Fulmars and Skuas, especially the latter; and many pilots had little experience of carrying out such attacks. But the new crash barrier fitted in *Ark Royal* (see Glossary) was impressive, greatly speeding up flying-on times and substantially reducing the time the force had to remain on a fixed course for recovery of the aircraft.

Describing the operation Somerville wrote:[18]

A shadower spotted us on the second day and our fighters shot him down. Yesterday we got another shadower but the weather was clear and the visibility maximum so he could hardly miss us. They came in one big wave – four sections of five bombers each. Our fighters engaged them as they came in but could not make any visible impression on them. A lot of the pilots were changed whilst *Ark* was at home and the new lot are still pretty green. Our AA fire as they came over was damned bad and I was very angry. Of course this is just an odd collection of ships that have never worked together so what can you expect. My ships are always being changed so I never get a chance to work them up. I think we brought down one of the bombers because he was seen diving steeply towards the sea but we did not actually see him crash in. What with the bombs falling all around you can't watch individual incidents very closely and I have to keep my wits about me to see that the fleet is on the right course to bring all guns to bear and that we keep as much as possible under our destroyer screen so that no U-boats will get a shot in.

He added:

> I forgot to say that early in the morning we delivered a bombing attack on Cagliari. It is a weird sight seeing the Swordfish all lined up in the pitch dark. As they start their engines they give out beastly sparks and flashes which you feel sure will be spotted by some Iti surface craft or U-boat, and one is on tenterhooks until the whole party is off. Having seen and talked to the pilots and observers before they took off one waits anxiously for their return and it is a joyous feeling when you have counted them back. Then comes the ticklish job of flying them on. You have to keep an eye cocked all the time for fear that the enemy may come and attack when you are stuck to one course, i.e., straight in the wind's eye and therefore have no freedom of manoeuvring.

Somerville transferred his flag back to *Renown* on 13 November when she returned from her Atlantic duty of covering convoys against attack by *Admiral Scheer*. In order to avoid any contact with the shore which might disclose the object of the next operation, *Argus* anchored in Gibraltar Bay after dark on 14 November on arrival from Britain, to fuel and unload stores. Force H comprising *Renown, Ark Royal, Argus, Sheffield, Despatch* and eight destroyers sailed before dawn to fly off more Hurricanes for Malta. The bad weather was far from ideal for operating aircraft. But the poor visibility made it likely that the force would not be detected and Somerville cancelled the planned attack on Alghero aerodrome in Sardinia which would have revealed its presence. Reports from Malta indicated that an Italian battleship, seven cruisers and a number of destroyers were concentrating south of Naples. Somerville suspected that they might be set on engaging Force H with superior forces to make up for their recent losses at Taranto, and decided to fly off the Hurricanes as far to the westward as weather conditions permitted. Two Skuas and twelve Hurricanes were flown off in the early morning of 17 November. At the time the wind was 20 knots at 2000 feet from the west and the latest forecast from Malta reported the wind in the Malta channel as south-west. As the range of the Hurricanes in still air was 521 miles and the distance to be flown 400 miles, it was felt there was a reasonable margin of safety. A Sunderland met the first flight north of Galita Island not far from Bizerta but a Glenn Martin failed to rendezvous with the second flight. Somerville was deeply concerned to learn that only one Skua and four Hurricanes arrived at Malta; a subsequent inquiry established that the pilots had not been adequately trained in respect of the range and endurance of their aircraft.[19] During this operation the cruiser *Newcastle* made a solo passage through to Malta. While the force was returning to Gibraltar the Admiralty reported that the *Admiral Scheer* was thought to be in the Azores area and ordered *Renown* and *Ark Royal* to steam at maximum speed to Gibraltar to refuel and thence proceed to the Azores. But as the fleet was about to enter Gibraltar Bay early on 19 November the instructions were cancelled.

Action off Cape Spartivento

The greatest importance was attached to the next operation to be carried out in the Mediterranean. This was to pass three MT ships carrying an urgently needed armoured brigade to the Middle East and two cruisers carrying 1400 RAF and Army personnel to Alexandria (codeword Collar). It was the most ambitious operation yet planned and it had become all the more important in the wake of Italy's declaration of war on Greece. Somerville considered it very likely that the Italian Fleet would intercept the convoy with major forces to compensate for the heavy losses sustained in the Mediterranean Fleet's recent attack at Taranto. He asked for the battleship *Royal Sovereign*, in Gibraltar for repairs, to be added to the force, but she was urgently needed to join the north Atlantic escort force. He was also anxious that the vigilance and fighting efficiency of his ships should be at its highest and was concerned that during the last month, in addition to routine patrols and escort duties, destroyers of the 8th and 13th Flotillas had taken part in both operations in the Mediterranean. Some rest and repair were essential for these ships. But to his 'fury' the Admiralty chose this moment to order that a French convoy be intercepted.[20] Despite Somerville's representations the Government insisted that the task be carried out, provided the convoy operation was not delayed. The cruiser *Despatch* and two destroyers sailed on 22 November and successfully returned with a merchant ship in company.

The operation was the first attempt to pass a small convoy of fast ships direct from Gibraltar to Alexandria. The troops for passage arrived in Gibraltar in the *Franconia*. To preserve the secrecy of the operation not more than 200 personnel were allowed to be seen on deck during daylight hours from the time of passing Tarifa Point in the Straits until the troops were transferred in harbour, after dark, to the cruisers. No inter-ship or shore communication was allowed. Troops were to be embarked in cruisers, 660 in *Manchester* and 760 in *Southampton*. These large numbers, each about the size of a cruiser's complement, meant that the ships were not in a fit condition to fight. But while the safe passage of personnel was to be given priority over the safe passage of the MT ships, there was an overriding consideration that, if Italian surface forces were sighted, the action taken by warships carrying RAF or Army personnel had to be the same as if they were not onboard. Four new corvettes were also to accompany the eastbound force.

Force H, consisting of *Renown*, *Ark Royal*, *Sheffield*, *Manchester*, *Southampton* and eight destroyers, sailed on 25 November. The plan was for the force to rendezvous with the battleship *Ramillies*, cruisers *Berwick* and *Newcastle* and five destroyers from the Mediterranean Fleet south of Sardinia. The combined force would escort the convoy to a position between Sicily and Cape Bon, the north-eastern tip of Tunisia, when Force H with *Ramillies* and two of the cruisers would return to Gibraltar, the remainder making the hazardous passage through the Narrows in darkness. The four corvettes were detached later the next day, having been unable to keep up with the convoy.

The following day, 27 November, *Ark Royal*'s aircraft sighted an Italian battlefleet of two battleships, six cruisers and seven destroyers about 40 miles to the north. With its battleships – of the Littorio class (equivalent to a Nelson) and of the Cavour class (the same age as *Renown* and similarly modernised) – the Italian fleet outmatched the British force. *Ramillies* and her group approaching from the east were then 90 miles away. *Ark Royal* was ordered to fly off a striking force and attack the Italian fleet. The enemy altered course to the eastward, pursued by *Renown* at 28 knots with all cruisers and destroyers disposed on a line of bearing 040°. *Ramillies*, which had been steering towards *Renown*, likewise altered course to the north-east to avoid losing ground in the chase, but was later ordered to join *Renown* lest a turn towards her by the enemy bring her under concentrated fire. At noon three Zara class cruisers were sighted to the northward; the two battleships identified as *Vittorio Veneto* and *Giulio Cesare* were then 27 miles distant. An overheated bearing forced *Renown* to reduce her speed to 27 knots; *Ramillies* was some distance astern. Fire was opened by the enemy 8-inch cruisers at 1221 and returned by the British cruisers and *Renown*, firing at 27,000 yards. The Italian cruisers and destroyers withdrew behind dense smoke. *Renown* sighted the two enemy battleships at 1250, which turned away, and she continued to close at maximum speed; *Ramillies*' best speed was only 20.7 knots. Heavy smoke prevented accurate fire during the chase. It was estimated that the enemy had a 3-knot advantage in speed over *Renown*, and firing stopped when the enemy drew out of range. At this point no reports of *Ark Royal*'s air strike had been received. It was evident that the enemy's speed had not been materially reduced, and there was no hope of catching up.

Force H was now steaming at high speed towards the enemy coast, only 30 miles distant and in close proximity to the air, submarine and light-force base at Cagliari. It was possible that the enemy withdrawal was a premeditated move to draw Force H into a dangerous area. If any ship was damaged the support of the whole force would be needed to extricate it, which would entail neglecting the main aim of the operation, and the convoy would have to proceed unescorted through the Narrows. Moreover enemy cruisers and destroyers to the north-west might already be working round towards the convoy and *Ark Royal*. As the Italian fleet was outside gun range, only a second air torpedo strike could reduce its speed, but this could not take place until after the enemy was under cover of the shore defences of Cagliari. It was not possible for *Renown* to engage two battleships with any chance of success, and if she had been able to catch up with the enemy force, *Ramillies* would still have been 30–40 miles away. Somerville therefore discontinued the chase. In the gun action *Berwick* received two hits, killing one officer and six ratings. There was no other damage to the force. A second Swordfish strike was sent off later in the afternoon, attacking a group of cruisers and shooting down a floatplane. A Skua strike also bombed three Italian cruisers.

In the afternoon there were two air attacks. The first was by ten Italian aircraft at 13,000 feet; fighter interception caused a number of bombs to be jettisoned at some distance from the fleet, but the enemy formation was not broken, and some bombs narrowly missed a destroyer on the screen. The second attack, carried out in three waves each of five aircraft at 14,000 feet, was directed on *Ark Royal*. There were several near-misses among the thirty bombs that fell around the ship, entirely obliterating her with enormous columns of water, but she emerged untouched. That evening the British forces split as arranged, the convoy continuing to Malta and Force H sailing back to Gibraltar. The complex operation had been a success. The convoy had got through unscathed and an attack by a superior force had been repulsed. Force H was greeted with cheers and bands playing on return to harbour, and there were congratulatory signals from Cunningham and from Malta. The engagement became known as the 'Action off Cape Spartivento', the southernmost point of Sardinia (to be distinguished from the other Cape Spartivento at the toe of Italy).

Six weeks earlier Somerville had returned after the Dakar débâcle to be shocked by the Admiralty's accusation against North. This time he was astonished to be told on his return that the Admiralty had ordered a board of inquiry into his handling of the action and that an Admiral of the Fleet, the Earl of Cork and Orrery, was on his way out by destroyer to conduct it. Criticism was not unexpected, but Somerville was infuriated that the inquiry had been ordered before any report of the action had been made and before the facts were known. It was Churchill who had instigated the proceedings.

He was firmly of the view that in all circumstances the strategic importance of attacking the enemy's battlefleet was an overriding consideration. He had also been vexed by Somerville's agonised reluctance to sink the French ships at Oran and subsequently by his continual questioning of policies for dealing with French ships and his support for North. There was now additional reason to get rid of him. The First Lord therefore ordered the inquiry with the support of the First Sea Lord, despite opposition from others in the Admiralty. Later, in letters to Cunningham, Pound wrote that he had 'felt like a pricked balloon when I read FO(H)'s signal that he had given up the chase and was going back to the convoy', and he harked back to the failure in August 1914 in bringing *Goeben* to action on its escape to Turkey, which 'set a very low standard in the conduct of naval operations. Harwood's conduct of affairs at the Plate and your conduct of operations in the Mediterranean put it back on a high plane again, and I can't afford that anything should again lower it.'[21] This would seem to carry more weight than the suggestion that Pound had decided on the inquiry in the confident expectation that it would justify Somerville and thereby thwart Churchill's aim.[22]

Somerville's case at the inquiry can be summarised in the point he made in his formal letter to the Admiralty: that the action had been fought against a superior enemy force which had been driven off at the very approaches to his defended base. 'Being satisfied that his main forces could no longer threaten the safety of my convoy, and incidentally that I had no reasonable chance of bringing his battleships to action, I had returned to the convoy as soon as possible in order to ensure the achievement of what the Fighting Instructions describe as the only object in convoy defence, namely the safe and timely arrival of the convoy at its destination.' He then described the reaction of his captains and officers, speaking of the indignation they felt about the inquiry and 'the bitterness of officers and men asking how it is that an action in which they took part and in which they succeeded in driving off and inflicting damage on a superior force of the enemy is now regarded as almost a defeat than a victory'. He ended his robust letter with the pointed comment: 'Their Lordships may well have failed to appreciate the full consequences of this action on their part.'[23] The board of inquiry, having established the facts, entirely upheld Somerville's conduct of the action. Not only was Somerville incensed by the Admiralty's action, Cunningham too thought it scandalous and regarded it as intolerable that commanders should continually be under threat of a board of inquiry.[24] The only good thing to come out of the affair was that it strengthened the bond between the men of Force H and their Admiral. A week later, Somerville spent the day in *Ark Royal*, as he said in his report, both to renew and refresh his flying experience and 'by climbing to high altitudes to rid my system of poison which recent events might have engendered'. He ended, 'this was fully achieved', to show that he considered the matter closed.[25]

Later, looking to the future when similar reinforcements might have to be escorted through the Mediterranean, Somerville gave further thought to the conflicting requirements of protecting a convoy and engaging the enemy. He sought from the Admiralty clarification of its conclusion to the inquiry, the wording of which implied that the ultimate object of British naval forces, namely to destroy the main enemy forces whenever and wherever met, should be the primary object even in convoy defence, irrespective of conditions. It seemed to him that this was hardly the intended meaning as it was opposite to the accepted practice of naval warfare. If it was indeed intended, then Clause 625 of the Fighting Instructions, which required 'the safe and timely arrival of the convoy at its destination' to be the primary object of his operation, should be amended. In reply the Admiralty confirmed that the extent to which it is justifiable to risk the safety of a convoy in order to engage enemy surface forces must depend on a balance being struck between the importance of, and the risk to, the convoy, and the importance of the enemy forces in relation to the general conduct of the war. Although this reply did not cover the point whether the prospect of destroying important units was favourable or otherwise, it appeared to him that no change of principle or accepted practice was intended. He now judged that, providing the present degree of control of sea communications could be maintained, it was the military and air situation in the central and eastern Mediterranean at the relevant time that should determine the priority. He noted that on no occasion to date had he had sufficient forces to ensure the safe passage of reinforcements and simultaneously to engage the enemy's main forces.

Somerville's fears that his actions might be misunderstood were well founded. With a Prime Minister insistent on giving the highest priority at all times to engaging the enemy battlefleet, there was always the possibility of a commander being charged with failing to bring the enemy to action. This was to be demonstrated six months later in the aftermath of the *Bismarck* operation, when Churchill called for courts martial – in the event unsuccessfully – in respect of the initial engagements in that action, a part of the operation in which Force H was not involved and which is not discussed in this book. There was also a precedent for Somerville's concern. In October 1914 when Admiral Jellicoe was Commander-in-Chief of the Grand Fleet and Churchill the First Lord of the Admiralty, Jellicoe sought to protect his conduct in future action with the enemy. His policy was that if U-boats accompanied the High Seas Fleet and that fleet turned away in an engagement, he would assume that it was the intention to lead his own ships over mines and submarines, and he would decline to be so drawn. This might be deemed a refusal of battle and a failure to bring to action as soon as it is expected. In his historic letter to the Admiralty Board he set out his thinking and policies on how to deal with these circumstances.[26] He was anxious to make his position clear because at that time the Admiral involved in the *Goeben* incident, referred to by Pound, faced a court martial for failing to pursue the enemy ship. Jellicoe was assured of the Board's full confidence in his contemplated conduct of the fleet; even so, he saw fit to send a copy of his letter and the original of the Admiralty's reply to his bank for safe keeping.[27] At Spartivento, Somerville faced dissimilar but comparable circumstances in that he felt he was being lured away from his main charge, the convoy, into an area dangerous for his ships, and thereby also allowing other Italian units to attack the convoy.

THE END OF THE YEAR

Two Italian submarines which had taken refuge in Tangier in a damaged condition in November were reported to have sailed on 13 December. A/S trawlers and destroyers were sent to patrol the vicinity, and to hunt to the west of Cape Spartel. The force available for this was much reduced by four destroyers being required elsewhere for Operation Ration. In that encounter *Forester* boarded a French steam trawler, which was brought into Gibraltar without incident. Destroyers were recalled and Ration suspended for Force H's next operation. In anticipation of a German force attempting to capture the Azores, either by a seaborne expedition or by transport aircraft, probably setting out from Bordeaux, *Renown*, *Ark Royal* and six destroyers sailed on 14 December to patrol off the islands. Three days later the force was ordered to return to Gibraltar at best speed, arriving there on 19 December.

The next operation required Force H to meet and escort westwards a force coming from the eastern Mediterranean – the battleship *Malaya*, two MT transports and five destroyers. Five destroyers of the 13th DF sailed from Gibraltar early on 20 December to carry out an anti-submarine sweep to the east ahead of the force and to cover the eastbound force from Skerki Bank in the Sicilian Narrows back to the rendezvous. *Renown*, *Ark Royal*, *Sheffield* and six destroyers sailed later in the day to the westward, reversing course when it was dark to pass through the Straits at night, the whole force joining up in the morning. The westbound force was met next day, 22 December. During its passage, the destroyer *Hyperion* was mined off Cape Bon and sank. Both forces returned to Gibraltar in company. The operation passed without incident in the western basin. The force was not detected – the result, Somerville believed, of the initial movement to the westward on leaving Gibraltar, the high-speed approach to the eastward and the low visibility unfavourable to air reconnaissance when south of Sardinia. The mining of *Hyperion* prompted Cunningham to order ships in future to steer a steady course and not zig-zag when passing through the Narrows.

The force arrived back in port late on Christmas Eve and expectations were high for a Christmas Day in harbour. But it was not to be. The German cruiser *Admiral Hipper* sailed from Germany into the Atlantic in early December to attack shipping. *Hipper* gained contact with convoy WS 5A of twenty ships about 700 miles west of Cape Finisterre in north-west Spain, and attacked the convoy at first light on Christmas Day. She was surprised to find the convoy heavily escorted by three cruisers, who drove her off but then lost touch in the prevailing low visibility. After breakfast that morning, Somerville had visited each ship of Force H in turn to wish them a Happy Christmas and to say how glad he was they were in harbour on such a filthy day; it was blowing hard and raining torrents. Just as he was starting to walk round the mess decks in *Renown* he received the signal of the *Hipper*'s attack and ordered steam for full speed while continuing his rounds. Instead of sitting down to Christmas dinner Force H went to sea. Somerville felt very sorry about this disruption to the men's plans, 'because they do enjoy their bit of fun on Christmas Day and they don't get much fun these days'. In his report he said he 'was gratified to observe the fine spirit in which the order to proceed to sea on Christmas Day was carried out. Ships remaining in harbour cheered those that were leaving and these cheers were returned with great heartiness. The order to close up at action stations was obeyed with even greater alacrity than usual.'[28] Paper hats were worn on some destroyers' bridges. The cheerfulness was not perhaps unexpected, bearing in mind the customary mess-deck rounds in a destroyer in harbour on Christmas Day during the war.

The Commodore of the convoy had ordered it to scatter when the enemy was sighted, and other ships including one of the groups hunting for the *Scheer* had been called in to try and round them up. Somerville was instructed to take charge of the very confused situation. It was not an easy task; he did not know of the positions of any of the ships or what they were doing, and they did not reply to his signals. They were apparently scattered over a wide area, each making for one of three different positions. Reconnaissance by nine planes from *Ark Royal* to a depth of 140 miles reported no sightings. By 2200 only three ships had been located.

Somerville asked the Admiralty to broadcast on commercial wave instructions to the ships to proceed to position 37° N 16° W. To add to his difficulties he was told during the night that the *Empire Trooper* with 2500 troops on board was in trouble, position also unknown. *Renown* and *Ark Royal* steamed at best speed to look for her while *Sheffield* and the destroyers rounded up the convoy. There was very low visibility and the bad weather restricted the amount of flying. To make matters worse *Renown's* starboard bulge (a protective outer hull), below the waterline, tore away about 30 feet from the fore end, and was beating the ship's side. Water was entering the mess decks fast and the ship's side was working in an ominous manner, with the result that speed had to be reduced to 18 knots. In due course other ships collected some of the scattered convoy, including the five MT ships scheduled to take part in the important convoy operation Excess to be launched shortly from Gibraltar; and ships were standing by the *Empire Trooper*. Force H returned to Gibraltar and *Renown* immediately docked for seven days' repairs to her hull. The sailing of the convoy was delayed by these events. The *Hipper*, which had been damaged by the gunfire from cruisers escorting the Atlantic convoy, returned to Brest.

The year was to end with Somerville being given the task to which he had most objection, another dose of Operation Ration, the interception of a French convoy. He submitted that if the operation was carried out it was likely that the French would re-establish air reconnaissance of the areas east and west of the Straits, in which case his proposed action to cover the movements of Force H and the Mediterranean convoy about to sail would be of little avail. Moreover Gibraltar was particularly vulnerable to air attack. At that time the ships in harbour included three capital ships, two aircraft carriers and the five large MT ships of the convoy. But the Admiralty insisted that the operation should continue. The cruiser *Bonaventure* and five destroyers sailed to intercept the French convoy of five merchant ships escorted by a trawler. The latter was permitted to proceed to Oran and the merchant ships brought to Gibraltar. Active obstruction of an armed boarding party on one of the ships resulted in a French passenger and a small girl being killed and four wounded. On 1 January 1941 the first French reconnaissance aircraft for some months appeared above the Rock, and again on 3 January, and was engaged by AA fire. These consequences persuaded the Admiralty to agree at once to Somerville's request to stop the operation and allow the destroyers time for rest and repair. As he noted, 'formerly I got just a direct snub'.

On his departure from Gibraltar at the end of the year Admiral North was given a great send-off by Force H, reflecting the friendship and mutual respect between the two admirals. He was relieved by Vice Admiral Sir George Edward-Collins, with whom Somerville did not enjoy the same rapport.

In contrast to the enemy's sweeping successes in Europe, and the increasing toll of shipping losses in the Atlantic, the situation in the Mediterranean at the end of the year was not unfavourable to Britain. The occasional use of the direct through route by fast convoys bound for Egypt had proved practicable and the ability to reinforce Malta, and hence the Middle East, by flying off fighters in the western Mediterranean had been demonstrated. There was quiet satisfaction that air attacks by the Italian Air Force could be mastered. In the eastern basin the Fleet Air Arm's attack on Taranto in particular had demonstrated the supremacy of the Mediterranean Fleet. The Army of the Nile's offensive was still driving victoriously westward, collecting hordes of Italian prisoners as it went.[29]

At times in those first few months Somerville must have felt the dice were loaded against him. He had the difficult job of trying to establish an effective fighting force and carrying out operations in enemy-air-controlled waters in a new and untried form of naval warfare. Diverting him from this major task were the continued demands of dealing with French ships, warship and merchant ships, which involved changes of plan and often wild-goose chases, against a background of uncertain or conflicting policies derived from what he saw as the Government's unnecessary hostility to the French. The tendency in London not to appreciate the naval implications of political decisions put Somerville out of sympathy with the Board of Admiralty, and a strained relationship developed between him and the First Sea Lord, and particularly with the Vice Chief of Naval Staff, Vice Admiral Tom Phillips, whose judgements Somerville considered lacked any understanding of how air power had changed the nature of war at sea. He felt this most strongly in the blow dealt to the morale of his force by the setting up of the inquiry after the action off Cape Spartivento, and reckoned that there was no frankness and no real confidence between the Admiralty and himself.[30] Matters were not left to his judgement; instead he was subject 'to carping criticism'.[31] He unburdened himself of much of the pressures and frustrations of the day in his letters to his wife. He professed no ambition or craving for glory, but wanted to do the best he could for his country without thought of personal consequences. After Spartivento he wrote, 'If they don't think I am the right man for the job they had better get rid of me.'

Unknown to him this very course of action had been determined upon two months earlier. In September, at a time when French diversions occupied centre stage and were causing friction between Somerville and London, the Admiralty decided to relieve him.[32] But it was not until the following January that the Board acted on this decision. The destroyer *Foresight* bringing out the new Captain of *Renown*, Captain R. R. McGrigor, also brought a letter addressed to Somerville.[33] The Admiralty did an about-turn, however, and signalled to the destroyer on passage instructing that the envelope was not to be delivered but was to be sent back unopened. This signal was intercepted in *Renown* but was not received in *Foresight*, and the letter was duly handed over to *Renown*. Somerville suspected that it might be telling him he was to be relieved and that the First Sea Lord now had second thoughts, or that his being relieved might be wrongly associated with the Spartivento inquiry. With tongue in cheek he signalled the Admiralty that a certain envelope had been received but he had an idea they did not wish him to open it, and requested instructions. He was told in reply that if the letter had been opened he was to consider the action required by it to be in abeyance; otherwise it was to be returned unopened. A few months later his suspicions were confirmed when he learnt that the letter was to tell him he was to be relieved by Admiral Harwood. Somerville was firmly convinced that it was his objections to the Government's French policy, which he never missed an opportunity of airing and which had been especially forceful in September, that caused his difficulties with Churchill and Phillips.

As has already been noted the Admiralty also decided, in October, that North should be relieved as a result of the passage of the French squadron through the Straits in September. That it was the intention then to relieve the two Admirals in command at Gibraltar was an indication of political confusion in London in dealing with the defeated French, and not of naval incompetence at Gibraltar in fighting the enemy with whom Britain was at war. Both Admirals had won and retained the confidence of the officers and men serving under them.

Somerville was also aware that Churchill disapproved of him and that, in anticipation of his being relieved after Spartivento, a number of flag officers had asked to be considered as his relief. He held it against his brother admirals that they did not stand up to Churchill even when, as also in North's case, 'they knew that something quite unfair and improper was being done'.[34] These circumstances must have made it difficult for him, but his resilience and good humour never weakened, and it is doubtful if more than a few close staff knew of this background or of his inner thoughts. He must have been cheered by a letter from the Fifth Sea Lord, Vice Admiral G. C. Royle, at the end of the year, who sent his 'heartiest congratulations on the way you have carried out quite the toughest and most difficult and tricky job any Flag Officer could ever have had. You have been magnificent …'[35]

The eagerness with which other flag officers offered themselves as replacements for Somerville can be explained. When Force H was formed so unexpectedly, it created a new sea appointment for a flag officer. In its first few months it had proved an ideal command. It was a squadron working independently in an active theatre of war and had already acquired a reputation in naval circles for its aggressive and fighting spirit. It is not surprising therefore that Somerville was envied for his plum job, nor that this might have been tinged with some resentment that a retired officer should be occupying a post which an active-service officer felt was his due. Among those putting their names forward was Phillips himself, the Vice Chief of Naval Staff, recognised by Somerville as the person striving hardest to get him relieved. But while Somerville may have had his detractors outside the force, it was a very different matter within his squadron. There is no better way of describing the esteem in which he was held than by quoting from a letter written to him by his nephew, a lieutenant in the Fleet Air Arm, after Somerville had spent a day at sea in *Ark Royal* in December:[36]

> Your visit made a tremendous impression on everybody and acted as a real tonic to all of us. The general view I have heard expressed by FAA [Fleet Air Arm] officers is that the ship is now operating under a Flag Officer who not only understands the general aspect of naval aviation but who had also taken the trouble to investigate the practical and personal side of it, and thus understand the small difficulties which sometimes appear so trivial and yet which are, in reality, so important. Most of us have suffered at one time or another under Flag and Commanding Officers who were abysmally ignorant of what an Observer or Pilot really did when he stepped into an aeroplane, and life is so much more pleasant now working under somebody who really understands.

His letter continued:

> If the Officers are pleased with your visit, the Air Gunners are more than delighted, and I have heard expressions of unbounded astonishment and admiration on all sides. You have shamed quite a few of my own Air Gunners who after a year of flying experience, consistently fail to establish W/T with their ship or other aircraft. The Engine Room Department too are extremely pleased that you managed to find time to have a look round down below and the remarks which

you apparently made about the cleanliness were very much appreciated.

Perhaps I shouldn't write all this, but I am doing so because I have never seen or heard of so much genuine enthusiasm aroused among all sections of the Ship's Company and I must find an outlet for my own enthusiasm and admiration.

Within six months of the formation of the force, the seeds of Somerville's leadership had already borne fruit. His readiness to stand by his captains and support them and the air striking forces, his practice of flying with the aircrews whenever he had the chance, his insistence on taking the blame for the passage of the French ships through the Straits and the Admiralty's unfairness in taking him to task over the Spartivento action further endeared him to all in his Command. His popularity was enormous, but it did not come at the expense of strict standards. Describing how a darkened ship had passed through the screen at night and ahead of the main body without being reported, he wrote: 'my damned destroyers never spotted her and *Renown* was slow in dealing with the situation, so raspberries have been flying pretty freely as you can imagine'.

Somerville was worried that his ships were not being given enough time to exercise and work up their fighting efficiency, nor to be trained to work together as a force. No other admiral had the experience he had gained at Dunkirk of the inability of ships to work close to enemy shores unless they had control of the air; and he knew the risks. He used every opportunity available, especially on return from operations and before entering harbour, to carry out gunnery, anti-submarine and other exercises, and periodically visited *Ark Royal* and flew from the ship. As an acknowledged authority on radar he was well suited to lead the Navy into the new era of air defence of the Fleet. Not that he was given adequate means of doing so: *Ark Royal*'s fighters, the 225mph Skuas and later the 265mph Fulmars, were no match for the German 350mph Me 109s and 110s which Force H would shortly encounter. This was a legacy of RAF control of naval aviation, which had persisted until it was handed over to the Admiralty in May 1937; the RAF had priority in production of fighters and bombers and the neglected British aircraft industry could not satisfy the needs of both services.[37]

Another continual worry at sea was the endurance of the destroyers. With the high-speed steaming of fleet operations, especially when operating with a carrier, the period during which a destroyer could provide effective escort was a critical feature. Replenishing at sea, when ships could readily refuel while under way, was practicable to a limited extent. Some refuelling of the escorts was practised by *Renown* and *Ark Royal*, but was only possible from oilers in very calm conditions. When operating from Gibraltar in the Mediterranean this was not too grave a limitation, thanks to the comparatively short duration of operational sorties – although this was to change later in the war when Malta no longer had the fuel to replenish ships for their return passage to Gibraltar after delivering a Malta convoy. But in the wider expanses of the Atlantic it was a severe problem and destroyers often had to be sent to refuel, leaving the heavy units at risk. This might also occur when destroyers could not maintain the fleet's speed in heavy weather and had to drop out and return to harbour.

Despite these anxieties, Somerville's robust confidence was undiminished after half a year in his taxing new role, and he could feel sure that Force H would handle with growing effectiveness the hazards that 1941 would bring.

5

IN THE
ASCENDANT

IN THE MEDITERRANEAN

FOLLOWING THE HEAVY defeat of the Italians in Libya in December, the new year of 1941 opened in the Mediterranean with a great sense of optimism among British forces. But almost immediately the deployment of the Luftwaffe marked a change of fortune. Fliegerkorps X, veterans of the Norwegian campaign, including pilots specially trained in ship attack, were deployed to the theatre. The intelligence available to Somerville was that by mid-January the Germans had 160 long-range bombers, 20 bomber–reconnaissance, 150 dive bombers, 40 twin-engined fighters and 40–60 transports, of which the majority were probably in Sicily. It was likely they would be reinforced by a long-range bomber group of forty aircraft practised in minelaying. These aircraft operated independently from the Italian force in Sicily of forty-five bombers and seventy-five fighters, and the Italians had a further seventy bombers and twenty-five fighters in Sardinia.

The first operation of the new year was to involve the entire naval strength from both ends of the Mediterranean: the passage of a fast military convoy of five ships, four for the Piraeus carrying urgently needed stores for the Greek army, and one for Malta with an important cargo that included 4000 tons of ammunition. This convoy was the first of six to be sailed into the

Mediterranean from Gibraltar during the next twenty months, the first two of which were loaded with military supplies and the other four with relief stores for Malta. The risks in passing these vital convoys through the Mediterranean had to be accepted. The general plan was that they should arrive at the Skerki Channel at dusk, pass through the Sicilian Narrows in darkness and be within fighter-escort range from Malta at dawn. Because of the mining threat and the water being too narrow for *Ark Royal* to operate her aircraft, capital ships in the escort could not proceed further than the entrance to the Skerki Channel.

To maintain security of the convoy, the assumption was encouraged that the MT ships would sail to the Middle East on the long route round the Cape of Good Hope. Before sailing from England, masters were instructed to provide statements of provisions and fuel required for the Cape passage. The departure of the convoy from Gibraltar was disrupted when a violent south-westerly gale caused two of the MT ships to break their moorings inside the harbour, with *Northern Prince* being driven ashore. Her 400 passengers were transferred to *Bonaventure* and four destroyers on their way to join the Mediterranean Fleet. These ships and the convoy, now of four ships, sailed on the evening of 6 January, feinting to the westward and returning eastward through the Straits under cover of darkness. *Renown, Malaya, Ark Royal* and seven destroyers sailed next morning to join the convoy.

On 9 January *Ark Royal* and *Sheffield* went ahead to allow five Swordfish of 821 Squadron to be flown off in the dark for Malta; all aircraft arrived safely. Two cruisers, *Gloucester* and *Southampton*, and one destroyer from the Mediterranean Fleet now joined the convoy to reinforce its escort through the Narrows. Both cruisers cut mines with their paravanes after crossing the 200-fathom line. In the afternoon ten Savoias attacked the force down-sun at 11,000 feet. There were some near-misses but AA gunfire was effective and there was no damage or casualties in the ships. Earlier reports of Italian cruisers at sea proved unfounded, although they were thought to be in the area. The large volume of smoke given off by one of the transports threatened to disclose the presence of the force and was of particular concern to Somerville. Force H parted company with the convoy in the evening and returned to Gibraltar without incident.

The convoy with its escort passed through the Narrows at night and next morning, 10 January, was attacked by two Italian torpedo boats, one of which was sunk. Admiral Cunningham in *Warspite*, with ships of the Mediterranean Fleet including *Valiant* and *Illustrious*, met the convoy south of Malta. A destroyer on the screen was mined and had to be towed to Malta. The fleet was heavily attacked in the afternoon by Junkers 87s and 88s, including dive bombers, assisted by Italian torpedo and high-level bombers. This was the first appearance of the Luftwaffe in the Mediterranean. The German attacks were effective, concentrating on *Illustrious*, which received six hits from heavy bombs and near-misses; only her armoured deck saved her from destruction. Next day, when she was rejoining the convoy, similar attacks on the fleet achieved hits on *Gloucester* and *Southampton*, with the latter catching fire and having to be sunk. *Illustrious* was severely damaged and with difficulty reached Malta, where she was attacked again. Despite these casualties all four MT ships in the convoy reached their destinations.

The setback to the fleet's control of the central Mediterranean was plain and emphasised the need for more fighters to be sent to Malta and for more ships to be fitted with radar. The *Illustrious* was so severely damaged that she had to cross over to the USA for repairs and was out of action for a year. *Formidable*, intended to be a relief for *Ark Royal* in Force H, was sent instead to the Mediterranean to replace *Illustrious*. As a result of the damage sustained by *Gloucester* and the sinking of *Southampton,* the Admiralty asked for views on whether *Sheffield* or *Bonaventure* should replace *Southampton* in the Mediterranean Fleet. Somerville valued *Sheffield* in the working partnership with *Renown* and *Ark Royal,* especially in terms of fighter control from her radar; Cunningham preferred *Bonaventure* with her up-to-date AA armament to a heavier but less modern cruiser. Asked if he would rather retain a Skua squadron or exchange it with a Fulmar one, Somerville favoured Fulmars because of their higher speed for engaging the Luftwaffe, and because there would be few opportunities for using Skuas for offensive operations in the western basin. At this period only four destroyers were available for Force H and for local duties. Somerville also called for reinforcement of the dockyard staff so that defects could be dealt with quickly. On several occasions the force had been immobilised for lack of destroyers fit for sea.

THE ATTACK ON GENOA

Force H's next mission was to carry the offensive to the Italian mainland. Somerville proposed to bombard Genoa. At the end of January there were intelligence reports of possibly two battleships and one 8-inch cruiser at Genoa, and a similar force plus two or more 6-inch cruisers at Spezia, 40 miles from Genoa. The object of the operation was to destroy enemy battleships and cruisers present; to lower Italian morale; to divert Italian naval air activity to north Italy; and to damage industries, supplies, shipping and so on.[1] The bombardment would be preceded by an attack on the Tirso dam in Sardinia, which would act as cover for the main operation. The dam supported a large reservoir which supplied a third of the power of the island. The Admiralty approved the operation, regarding the risks involved to *Renown* and *Ark Royal* as fully justified. Cunningham also welcomed it as being likely to divert air forces from southern Italy and make it harder for the Italian Fleet to decide from which direction the coast might be threatened. There was also some information that an expedition, possibly against the Balearics, was being prepared at Genoa and the Admiralty wanted the bombardment to take place as soon as possible. The risks of detection during a moonlight approach were accepted.

Renown, Malaya, Ark Royal, Sheffield and ten destroyers sailed on 31 January. The weather had deteriorated on the morning of 2 February when eight Swordfish from 810 Squadron took off in the dark to attack the dam at dawn. The Admiralty assessment that there were 3 feet of concrete at the top of the dam and that it was probably not at all well defended with guns proved incorrect. The planes were met with heavy gunfire during the whole of their approach up the valley and there was exceptionally intense fire at the reservoir. Only three of the eight torpedoes dropped hit the dam; one aircraft failed to return, its crew being taken prisoner. That the Italians should have been so alert on a Sunday morning suggested a lapse of security, despite the stringent precautions taken on passage (see below), and this was attributed to loose talk in Gibraltar. There was no dam-busting to report and it was a disappointing start to the operation. The Swordfish had experienced severe icing at 5000 feet and the weather further deteriorated all day. Fleet speed had to be reduced to 15 knots, the maximum the destroyers could maintain without damage. *Ark Royal* was dipping her flight deck into the sea and the north-westerly gale limited ground being made to the north and west. To arrive off Genoa after dawn would have been unacceptable and the attack had to be abandoned.

The squadron sailed again the following week on 6 February to carry out that aborted operation, but this time it was to proceed direct to Genoa. Before sailing, Somerville was alarmed to learn that ratings ashore had told a rating in *Sheffield* that the force was going to Genoa. He considered this a criminal laxity of security and imposed a cover plan. Orders were issued for a sweep against French merchant ships in the western Mediterranean. *Resolution* was ordered to prepare boarding and steaming parties to embark in destroyers taking part in the operation. Genuine orders for the Genoa operation, now under a new codeword, were sent to commanding officers in sealed envelopes, which were not to be opened until they were at sea. The ships sailed in two groups. Six destroyers left harbour unobtrusively in units of one or two ships proceeding eastwards as if on patrol or exercising. *Renown, Malaya, Ark Royal* and *Sheffield*, screened by four destroyers, left later in the day. All groups joined up to make passage to the north-east at high speed. In order to remain undetected for as long as possible, they altered course to avoid detection by ships reported by *Ark Royal* aircraft on anti-submarine patrols and by fighters. If an aircraft was spotted by radar, course was immediately altered to the south or east to give the impression that the objective was a town in Sardinia. The force was sighted by French aircraft and by a civil aircraft flying from Majorca to Marseilles. The ships passed between Ibiza and Majorca on the night of 7 February and feinted towards Sardinia in daylight next day. *Jupiter* and *Firedrake* were detached to make a W/T diversion east of Minorca by transmitting confusing signals. To encourage the deception that Sardinia was the target, it was proposed that the RAF at Malta should bomb Cagliari or Algheri airfield in the north of Sardinia, but no aircraft were available.

At this time and unknown to Somerville, the Italian Fleet had put to sea. Admiral Iachino, Commander-in-Chief afloat of the Italian Navy, had been informed at once of Force H's departure from Gibraltar on 6 February, but there had been no compromise of security on its mission and the Italians were left guessing. He sailed from Spezia at 1900 on 8 February with three battleships and seven destroyers, ordering three 8-inch cruisers from Messina to join him next morning 40 miles west of Cape Testa, the northernmost point of Sardinia. Thereafter the force would cruise westward and await reports from air reconnaissance. During the night the two opposing forces were steaming towards each other. Ignorant of the other's presence, they passed a bare 50 miles apart.

At 0400 on 9 February *Ark Royal* with three destroyers was detached to carry out air attacks on Leghorn and Spezia. At 0505 a striking force of fourteen Swordfish was flown off; these were followed by four more carrying magnetic mines and later by spotting aircraft for the bombarding ships with fighter escort. The oil refinery at Leghorn was attacked with bombs and incendiaries. Surprise was achieved, as only one or two guns opened fire when the attack started, but a few minutes later the AA fire became severe. Two of the striking force mistook their landfall and attacked alternative targets at Pisa aerodrome and railway junction. The minelaying aircraft dropped mines in the eastern and western entrance to Spezia harbour. All aircraft returned safely except one brought down over Leghorn; its crew were taken prisoner.

The bombarding ships made an accurate landfall off Genoa, vital to the success of the operation. There was no sign of any activity from shore and no other ships were in sight. Spotting aircraft reported no battleships present. *Renown* and *Malaya* opened fire with their 15-inch guns at 0714 from about

10 miles off the coast. Throughout the bombardment nothing could be seen of Genoa and the firing was carried out using indirect fire with aircraft spotting. *Renown*'s opening salvoes were quickly spotted on to the Ansaldo Works, marshalling yards and factories on both sides of the Torrente Polcevera. Explosions and fires were seen in this area. A big fire was started near the commercial basin and a merchant ship was hit. A salvo falling near the power station caused an especially violent explosion and an oil tank was set on fire. Salvoes also fell in the area west of Ponte Daglio Asscreto and an electrical works. The secondary armament engaged targets along the waterfront. *Malaya* fired on the dry docks and targets in the vicinity. Massive explosions were observed in the docks and among warehouses. The battleship *Diulio*, in dock, was straddled but not hit. *Malaya*, built during the First World War, was a present to the nation from the Federated Malay States, and it was the custom for the ship to fly the States' ensign whenever the ship was in action. The flag was not unlike that of a well-known shipping line and during the bombardment Somerville signalled to her, 'You look like an enraged P and O.' *Sheffield*'s fire was directed on to industrial installations on the left bank at the mouth of the Torrente Polcevera. Many fires and two big explosions were observed. After half an hour fire was checked and the ships steamed south at full speed to rejoin *Ark Royal*. During the bombardment *Renown* fired 125 rounds and *Malaya* 148 rounds of 15-inch shell, and *Sheffield* 782 rounds of 6-inch shell.

Somerville gave his own description of the bombardment to his wife:[2]

About 6.45 a dull smudge ahead of us showed the high mountains behind Genoa but it was terribly hard to be sure that we had hit the right part of the coast. Our luck was in and Martin Evans (navigating officer) got a fix, which showed we were just right. Not a sign from shore, not a ship except our own on the sea. We steamed up to the beginning of the run, i.e. about 10 miles off Genoa, and then flash went the broadsides. Of Genoa itself we could see nothing. Our guns were laid by gyro and our aircraft over the town spotted us on to the various targets. The first salvoes fell almost exactly where we wanted them and *then* I felt content.

The curtain was up and the tragedy was on. For half an hour we blazed away and I had to think of Senglea, Valletta [both Maltese towns that had suffered bombing raids], London and Bristol etc. to harden my heart. But I was watching the map and reports of the aircraft and I do believe that practically all of our salvoes fell on works, warehouses,

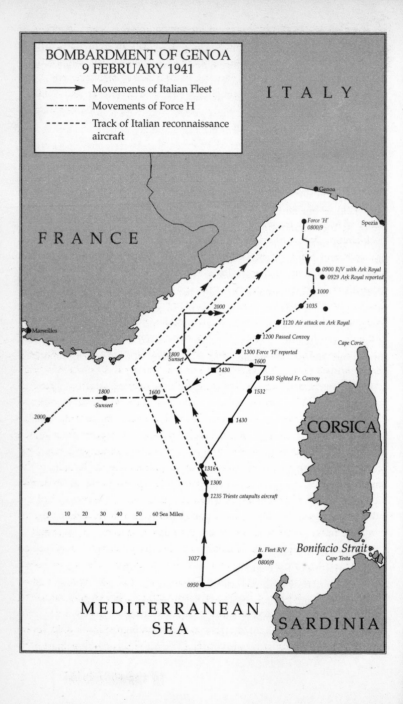

BOMBARDMENT OF GENOA
9 FEBRUARY 1941

→ Movements of Italian Fleet

─·─·─ Movements of Force H

─ ─ ─ Track of Italian reconnaissance
aircraft

ITALY

Genoa

Force 'H'
0800/9

Spezia

FRANCE

0900 R/V with Ark Royal
0929 Ark Royal reported
1000

1035

Marseilles

2000

1120 Air attack on Ark Royal

1200 Passed Convoy

1300 Force 'H' reported

Cape Corse

1800
Sunset

1600

1430

1540 Sighted Fr. Convoy

1532

1800   1600
Sunset

1430

2000

CORSICA

1316

1300

1235 Trieste catapults aircraft

0   10   20   30   40   50   60 Sea Miles

1027

It. Fleet R/V

0800/9

Bonifacio Strait
Cape Testa

0950

MEDITERRANEAN
SEA

SARDINIA

shipping, docks etc. Still it is no use pretending that some innocent people were [not] killed. War is lousy. After half an hour we turned away and steamed south at full speed to meet *Ark* who had been doing her stuff, blocking up the entrance to Spezia and plastering an all-important refinery at Leghorn that the RAF had never managed to hit yet. We made contact all right and again I gave a sigh of relief as were now able to meet the expected air attacks …

Two shadowing aircraft were shot down and an attack by two bombers was unsuccessful. But the continuing haze prevented bombers from locating the force. The wind was from astern and each time *Ark Royal*'s aircraft flew off or landed the force had to turn back towards the enemy air and surface bases. These were exactly the circumstances when pilots needed to have the highest deck-landing skills. Otherwise, as indeed happened, when a pilot made a poor approach and had to be waved round again, precious miles were lost in the urgent process of distancing the force from the enemy coast.

A hit-and-run raid of this type can be compared with attacks such as the German bombardment of Scarborough in the first winter of the First World War, where the enemy force may get in undetected but is more likely to be at risk on its return journey home. Still unknown to Somerville, the Italian Fleet was at sea looking for him to the west of Sardinia. It was well placed to apply the established principle of keeping between the enemy and its base. On hearing that Genoa had been bombarded, Iachino steamed north at speed to intercept, catapulting aircraft to search to the north-west within 20 miles of the French coast. He adjusted course later a few degrees westward, a course which would have ensured that he made contact. But reports from Italian reconnaissance aircraft persuaded him to alter course to the north-east. This led him mistakenly to a French convoy, in the process passing 30 miles to the southward of Force H. Although *Ark Royal* had fighters in the air there was bad weather and poor visibility and neither side knew of the presence of the other. As in December 1914, low visibility allowed the bombarding force to evade the heavy units of the homeland Navy deployed to cut off its retreat.[3]

The force arrived back in Gibraltar on 11 February. Complete surprise had been achieved, a tribute to Somerville's efforts to disguise the force's movements and intentions. Only one aircraft was lost. It seemed almost unbelievable that it should have been so successful. It was equally surprising that the Italians did not have some form of patrol on the approaches to Genoa. Somerville had been concerned that areas of civilian population should not be hit, and that desire appeared to have been fulfilled. The track of the force both to and from the target area had passed close to the Italian Fleet that was out looking for him. Somerville's guardian angel, to whom he had become accustomed to paying respectful homage, was evidently in a good mood. Everyone in the force was 'very cock-a-hoop' about the success of the raid, which caused much dismay to the enemy. There was anger and gloom among Italians that their country had allowed herself to be attacked in this way, the morale of the population being affected by a bombardment much more than by an air raid. In Britain the attack came as a very welcome piece of good news during a stressful period of the war, with the BBC reporting air raids every night, especially on Coventry, Portsmouth, Plymouth and Liverpool; it was also an anxious time for ships' companies when their hometowns were being hit. Churchill was delighted by Somerville's action and signalled to him, 'Congratulations on the success of your enterprise', adding, in a sting in the tail that reflected the earlier difficulties between them, 'which I am glad to see you organised.' To the country he broadcast with oratorical defiance: 'It is right that the Italian people should be made to feel the sorry plight into which they had been led by Mussolini. If the cannonades of Genoa, rolling along the coast, reverberating in the mountains, has reached the ears of our French comrades in their grief and misery, it may cheer them with a feeling that friends are active, friends are near, and that Britannia rules the waves.' Genoa was a personal success for Somerville and ended the rift between him and Churchill.

WESTWARD EMPHASIS

In early February the German battlecruisers *Gneisenau* and *Scharnhorst* successfully avoided Home Fleet patrols in the Denmark Strait between Iceland and Greenland, and reached the Atlantic at large. After sinking five ships recently dispersed from an outward-bound convoy off Newfoundland, the German ships moved to the Sierra Leone (SL) convoy routes. Force H was now to become involved in Atlantic operations for the next six weeks. In Gibraltar Catalina flying boats replaced Sunderland long-range reconnaissance aircraft and an Area Combined Headquarters was set up to improve air co-operation. It was not until much later in the year that work was started on extending the runway into the sea.

The day after the bombarding force returned from the Genoa expedition a raider report in the Atlantic was received. *Renown, Ark Royal, Sheffield* and five destroyers sailed at once on 12 February to give assistance to convoy HG 53. Subsequently the force was ordered to take over the escort of convoy WS 6 from *Rodney. Sheffield* was detached on 13 February to cover another convoy, SLS 64. Without her the force lacked radar cover to allow fighters to intercept

Focke Wolf four-engine Kondor aircraft carrying out long-distance maritime reconnaissance. In areas patrolled by these planes radio silence was strictly observed except when making an enemy sighting report. It was a severe restriction. On one occasion two out of five aircraft sent out for a search could not find the ship on return in the rapidly worsening visibility (this was before the airborne radar ASV became available), although searchlights were being pointed for their benefit. Eventually they had to request a D/F – direction-finding – bearing.

Renown and *Ark Royal* stayed with their convoy until 21 February when they were relieved by *Malaya*, and then set course for Gibraltar. On learning that a Hipper class cruiser might be preparing to leave Brest, they altered course to the north-east, but resumed passage when it was reported that the ship was still in dry dock. The force arrived back in Gibraltar on 25 February. The Admiralty announced that it intended to employ Force H on Atlantic trade routes in the near future and therefore commitments in the western basin should not be undertaken for the present.

On 8 March *Malaya*, escorting convoy SL 67, sighted the German battle-cruisers *Gneisenau* and *Scharnhorst*, who at once retired to the west. Force H was alerted and *Renown*, *Ark Royal*, *Arethusa* and two destroyers sailed the same day. The force steamed at 27 knots towards the Canaries, relieving *Malaya* who returned to Freetown. For nine days *Renown* remained in the centre of this fifty-five-ship 7-knot convoy, 'hardly moving', much to Somerville's undisguised impatience. The battlecruiser *Repulse* and the carrier *Furious*, also in the area, were placed under Somerville's orders, but as their limited endurance and low fuel meant that they could not deal effectively with potential attacks by the German ships, he ordered them to return to Gibraltar; *Furious* subsequently sailed for Britain. The two destroyers, unable to keep up in the adverse weather conditions, were also sent back.

Meanwhile the German ships had sunk sixteen ships from dispersed convoys. The Admiralty anticipated that they would return to Germany by the northern route through the Denmark Strait but ordered Force H north in case they made for Brest. On 20 March three ships captured by the Germans with prize crews on board were reported in the vicinity. When *Renown* approached *Bianca*, she was seen to be abandoning ship, and as the boats pulled clear scuttling charges exploded and fire broke out in the engine room and bridge. The boarding party nonetheless boarded her and managed to extinguish fires, but the ship was low in the water with a considerable list and nothing could be done to save her. A few hours later another ship, *San Casimoro*, was also abandoned and scuttling charges fired when *Renown* closed. While the boarding party was getting alongside an enemy report was received by V/S (visual signal) from a Fulmar at 1815 that the two enemy battlecruisers had been sighted north-west of *Renown*. The aircraft had sighted the ships 600 miles west-north-west of Cape Finisterre, but its wireless failed and Somerville received the report only as it passed *Renown* on returning to *Ark Royal*. Unfortunately the enemy's course was given as north, to which the ships had altered on being sighted, and the report did not say that they had initially been steaming north-east. This was not mentioned until after the aircraft had landed on. Nor did the carrier, separated from *Renown* by 20 miles, immediately signal this vital information to Somerville, who was thus deprived for some hours of intelligence which might have helped him assess correctly the battlecruisers' destination. At the time of sighting, the enemy was 110 miles to the north-west of *Ark Royal*. Shadowing aircraft could not reach the ships before dark, after which the chance of finding them would be remote. One Fulmar was sent as a forlorn hope but, after searching for two hours in pitch darkness and with clouds down to sea level, no contact was made. Conditions had not improved next morning and contact was not regained, to Somerville's intense disappointment. *Gneisenau* and *Scharnhorst* returned to Brest on 22 March. This was the first and only foray made by the battlecruisers against Atlantic shipping.

The force returned to Gibraltar, sailing again on 24 March to patrol off the Bay of Biscay to give cover to Atlantic convoys between the latitudes of Lisbon and Ushant. For the three weeks after the battlecruisers reached Brest almost the whole strength of the Home Fleet and Force H was disposed some 500 miles to the west, in case the enemy ships attempted to return home by the northern route. The two or three squadrons thus employed, each with at least one capital ship, returned one at a time to Scapa or Gibraltar to refuel, with Admiral Tovey, Commander-in-Chief Home Fleet, and Somerville alternating in command of the blockading force.[4] All available submarines were deployed off Brest. The RAF kept up a heavy bombing programme on the ships in Brest, and mines were laid in the approaches to the port. This blockade was reminiscent of the Napoleonic Wars, with capital ships patrolling to the westward and submarines and reconnaissance aircraft taking the place of the old Inshore Squadron of frigates.

Meanwhile in the Mediterranean *Sheffield* and four destroyers had sailed on 29 March to intercept a French convoy of four freighters, escorted by the Vichy French destroyer *Simoun*, carrying war materials including a cargo of rubber. *Sheffield's* orders were to take the rubber-laden ship to Gibraltar or, in the last resort, to sink her. The convoy, which was proceeding from

Vice Admiral Sir James Somerville KCB DSO *Imperial War Museum A3748*

Force H at Gibraltar – the hard core:

Renown (flagship August 1940 to July 1941)   *National Maritime Museum N6218*

Ark Royal in her usual berth   *National Maritime Museum N6228*

Sheffield   *National Maritime Museum N6253*

F Class destroyer *Forester* leaving harbour   *National Maritime Museum N6296*

French Fleet at Mers-el-Kebir *Imperial War Museum HU68018*

Cruisers *Berwick* (on horizon), *Southampton* and *Manchester* in action off
Cape Spartivento, November 1940 *Imperial War Museum A2347*

Ark Royal, Malaya, Renown off Gibraltar — the Genoa bombardment force,
February 1941 *Imperial War Museum A2579*

Swordfish Mk I
Imperial War Museum MH167

A Fulmar catching the arrestor wire on landing *Imperial War Museum A8351*

Club Run: *Ark Royal* flying off Hurricanes for Malta *Royal Naval Museum*

Club Run: *Argus* with Hurricanes on flight deck *Imperial War Museum A9543*

Club Run: the first Spitfires to be flown through, from *Eagle*, March 1942
Imperial War Museum A9583

Admiral Somerville with his Chief of Staff Captain P. William-Powlett *Imperial War Museum A6529*

German battleship *Bismarck* *Imperial War Museum HU3286*

Hermione, successor to *Sheffield* in Force H *Imperial War Museum A5742*

Nelson down by the bows after being torpedoed in Malta convoy, September 1941
Imperial War Museum A5641

Malaya, flagship from October 1941
Imperial War Museum A5462

ARK ROYAL TORPEDOED

The destroyer *Laforey* going alongside *Ark Royal* to pump over boiler feed water and supply power *Royal Naval Museum*

Casablanca to Oran, had been allowed to pass through the Straits without being stopped. *Sheffield* caught up with them in the Mers-el-Kebir area and ordered them to heave to for inspection. Instead they raced to get inside territorial waters and were pursued by the destroyers. Shore batteries opened fire and *Sheffield* fired warning shots. With the freighters now in territorial waters, the seizure of one cargo of rubber was not considered sufficient to justify the serious consequences that would result from an attack, and the ships withdrew. On return passage to Gibraltar the force was attacked by Vichy aircraft, which continued the bombing until the ships were off Europa Point. *Sheffield* was ordered to stay at sea to ensure that the bombers did not also attack ships in harbour.[5] The failure of the mission was criticised by the Admiralty, but the incident confirmed Somerville's view that seizure of French ships in territorial waters would most probably lead to reprisals. Although it was possible for Gibraltar-based forces to have a small nuisance effect on French trade, there were not enough surface or air forces to interfere with it to any serious extent. The French would call their bluff if there were any departure from the recognised procedure of limiting visit or search to vessels on the high seas or in enemy waters.

During this period, Force H's primary duty was to the westward in the Atlantic rather than to the eastward in the Mediterranean. It had been planned that *Furious* should take the place of *Ark Royal* for the ferrying of Hurricanes to Malta, thereby releasing the *Ark* to cover the Atlantic convoys while the threat from German warships remained. But the poor state of *Furious's* engines did not permit this arrangement and the force had to return to Gibraltar, sailing on 1 April to fly off twelve Hurricanes for Malta with two Skuas as escort. The very strong westerly gale prevented *Ark Royal* leaving her berth in the evening and the planned feint to the west had to be abandoned. *Argus* had brought the Hurricanes out to Gibraltar but they were transferred to *Ark Royal* because her longer flight deck and higher speed allowed the planes to carry more fuel, which meant they could be flown off at a greater distance from Malta. All aircraft arrived safely.

On passage back to Gibraltar Somerville learnt that the Government might decide to prevent *Dunkerque* leaving Mers-el-Kebir the following day, by torpedoing her without warning by submarines deployed for that purpose. Should this happen, an immediate and heavy air attack could be expected on Gibraltar and it was imperative that the harbour should be cleared of as many ships as possible. In the event the attack on *Dunkerque* did not take place. The force returned at 24 knots to refuel and store, and sailed a few hours later with *Furious*, recently arrived from Britain, into the Atlantic. Aircraft were exchanged between the two carriers, with ten Fulmars replacing nine of *Ark Royal*'s Skuas. A welcome addition were four new Swordfish fitted with ASV radar, one per squadron and one kept as spare. At 1000 feet this equipment could detect surface vessels at 10 miles, at 3000 feet 30 miles. Returning to harbour that night, 6 April, *Renown* and *Ark Royal* started a long-awaited and much needed four-day self-refit. But at midnight a signal was received that the two German battlecruisers might be leaving Brest and Force H put to sea at 0300. Somerville in *Renown* with *Ark Royal*, *Sheffield*, *Fiji* and three destroyers relieved Tovey in *King George V* and other Home Fleet ships. *Queen Elizabeth*, *Hood* and *Repulse* were also in the area. *Repulse* was detached to proceed to Gibraltar to refuel, rejoining on 14 April. Force H, having now established a remarkable record of sea time, returned to Gibraltar. The ships then reverted to long notice for steam for their refits. This coincided with a request from Cunningham that the force provide a diversion in the western basin for his intended bombardment of Tripoli on 21 April. Somerville regretfully had to reply that defects in his ships had now reached a stage when they seriously affected the efficiency of the force, and these could not be put right in time to sail on 19 April. The ships completed their self-refits without interruption.

Further reinforcements of ships for the Mediterranean Fleet and fighters for Malta were included in the next operation – another Club Run in the Mediterranean. The impending evacuation of British troops from Greece made it all the more urgent that there should be a minimum of delay in the passage of the ships. *Argus* brought out the Hurricanes to Gibraltar, where they were transferred to *Ark Royal*. *Renown*, *Ark Royal*, *Sheffield* and five destroyers sailed on 24 April, the transiting ships *Dido*, *Abdiel* and six destroyers feinting first to the west before entering the Mediterranean in the dark. With twenty-three Hurricanes on *Ark Royal*'s flight deck it had to be accepted that no flying of ship's aircraft was possible on the outward passage, but Fulmars were kept ranged forward and to starboard of the barrier ready to be catapulted should enemy bombers attack. Hurricanes' wings did not fold, so they could not be struck down into the hangar. To land on the Fulmars again after combat would have meant moving all the Hurricanes forward of the barrier and hoping that no Fulmar would make a bad landing and write off some of the Hurricanes destined for Malta. This was a high-risk venture. It was known at the time that German dive bombers had been transferred to Cagliari, and *Ark Royal* had only sixteen serviceable Fulmars available. The Hurricanes were flown off in three flights after dawn on 26 April each led by a Fulmar, and the ship reinforcements sailed at full speed to Malta keeping close to the African coast. All aircraft and ships arrived safely.

THE LAND CAMPAIGNS IN THE EASTERN MEDITERRANEAN

While Force H had been busy in the Atlantic, the military situation in the Middle East had changed dramatically. 1941 had started well, with the Army of the Nile's attack on the Italians in Libya. General O'Connor with his troops had advanced 500 miles, beyond Benghazi, and by mid-February had destroyed an Italian army of more than nine divisions at a cost of 2000 casualties. The port of Tripoli lay within his grasp. If he could take it, he would drive the Italians completely out of North Africa, thus achieving victory on an epic scale. But this was to be denied him. The Italian invasion of Greece in October 1940 had met with stubborn resistance. To help the Greeks defend their homeland, London decided to halt the British advance in North Africa and despatch troops to the Balkans. The bulk of O'Connor's successful army was withdrawn, leaving only a holding force. The initiative in Libya was lost. And it was at this time, in February 1941, that the Germans came to the rescue of their ally: General Rommel arrived in North Africa with two divisions to help the Italians. The attack by his Afrika Korps at the end of March swept the British out of Cyrenaica, recaptured Benghazi, took O'Connor prisoner and by the end of April had reached the Egyptian border. Only Tobruk held out. Malta now acquired greater significance. It was a base from which aircraft and submarines could harry and disrupt the enemy's shipping and transport supplying the armies in North Africa.

General Wavell, the British Commander-in-Chief in the Middle East, planned a new campaign to drive the enemy forces back and relieve Tobruk. Churchill hoped it would lead to the complete defeat of Rommel and the removal of Axis armies from North Africa. But towards the end of April, Enigma decrypts showed that Rommel was likely to be reinforced by a German armoured division. The British forces in Egypt were dangerously short of tanks and Churchill insisted on immediate reinforcements to be sent 'at all costs'. The risk of losing the vehicles or part of them on passage through the Mediterranean had to be accepted, but the personnel for the tanks would travel on the longer but safer route round the Cape. The operation, codeword Tiger, was subjected to maximum security. No one outside the highest circles was to know that some of the ships would turn off for Gibraltar; it was imperative that everyone in the convoy should think they were going round the Cape.[6] In support of the operation, fifteen Beaufighters flew through Gibraltar on 3 May en route for Malta to provide additional fighter escort for the operation.

The Admiralty indicated that a bombardment of Naples as part of the operation, even if only by a cruiser, might produce good results; much material for Tripoli was being shipped from the port. Somerville considered the suggestion quite impractical. The chances of surprising the enemy were low. The convoy would certainly be detected by Day 3 and alert the enemy, rendering the chances of carrying out the bombardment and escaping interception remote. The bombarding ships would have to leave the convoy about three hours before dark, depriving it of considerable protection against air attack, the chief danger on that day. It was not justified to risk the valuable *Ark Royal* in the Tyrrhenian Sea, and, without fighter protection, air spotting was unlikely to be of much service.[7] He believed that the scheme could have been put forward only by someone who had not yet appreciated the new and menacing situation produced by the arrival of the Luftwaffe in southern Italy. It forced him again into the uncomfortable position of having to reject a proposal for offensive action. For this he blamed Phillips, Vice Chief of Naval Staff, whom he looked upon as an armchair sailor regrettably enjoying the confidence of the Prime Minister as well as the First Sea Lord.[8]

The five 14½ knot MT ships in the convoy passed through the Straits during the night of 5 May. When formed up the next day the escort comprised Force H, consisting of *Renown*, *Ark Royal*, *Sheffield* and six destroyers; *Queen Elizabeth*, *Fiji*, *Naiad*, which were on their way to reinforce the Mediterranean Fleet; and *Gloucester*, *Kipling* and *Kashmir*, sent from the eastern Mediterranean to reinforce the convoy's escort through the Narrows after being prevented by mines from entering Malta. The very clear and calm weather aided detection by Italian reconnaissance planes. *Ark Royal* reported that at 10,000 feet the convoy could be seen in detail at 20 miles, and its smoke at a much greater distance. Nevertheless no attacks were made on the force on 7 May.

On 8 May the force was attacked by eight torpedo bombers, which dropped their torpedoes at 3500 yards just inside the destroyer screen – the first attack in a hectic afternoon and evening. Writing to North, Somerville gave a vivid description:[9]

We started off with an elaborate westward blind and a proper jigsaw of destroyer exchanges and refuelling. The MT ships were ships that pass in the night and as the result of this and also most favourable weather I don't believe the Itis had any idea until 0530 on Day 3. There *must* have been a flap then, but it was not until 1345 that the first attack came in. Eight or nine wicked looking brutes just skimming above the sea. They attacked my column and dropped their torpedoes at about

3500 yards just outside or inside the screen. One was shot down before he dropped, two crashed after dropping. Then we had to comb the tracks [see Glossary]. McGrigor (*Renown*) did this damn well but as we were combing one successfully the damn thing [torpedo] suddenly altered 90° to port and came straight for our bow. Now we're for it I thought but, would you believe it, the damn thing had finished its run and I watched it sinking about 10 yards from the ship.

For the operation *Ark Royal* carried only twelve instead of her proper complement of twenty-four Fulmars. After a very short time the number of serviceable aircraft had been reduced by combat to five; it was never more than seven. By rapid re-equipping and re-servicing a permanent patrol was maintained, varying in number from two to the full number that were still serviceable. During the attacks the Fulmars sighted three separate formations of sixteen Ju 87s, twelve Ju 88s and six Me 110s. Seven enemy aircraft were destroyed, four by AA fire and three by fighters; two were probably destroyed and at least three damaged. Two Fulmars were lost but the crew of one was saved. No hits by bombs or torpedo were obtained on the ships, but a gunnery accident in *Renown* killed six ratings and wounded one officer and twenty-five further ratings.

Somerville's description of the action continued:

We had intermittent attacks all afternoon. Luckily the cloud base was about 5000 feet and they *didn't* like it. We put up a hell of a fire and our Fulmars, at times reduced to two in the air, mixed it up magnificently. I can't say too much praise of the wonderful show they put up. The result was that except for one stick just ahead of *Ark* the bombing was ineffective. At 1830 we found some very large formations approaching from Sicily. Between 25 and 35 dive bombers with 8 or 10 Me 100s escorting them. Up went all our six fighters (all we had left because another had crashed and others were shot up). They mixed it up so well that a lot of the JUs dropped their bombs miles away. The whole party disappeared to the west and then returned to the east but carried on home and never attacked us. By this time we were right in the entrance to the Skerki Channel and I had to turn the force west – time 2015 – as the water was too narrow for the *Ark* to operate. We'd hardly finished turning when three T/B [torpedo bomber] aircraft attacked from right ahead, i.e. from the west. The three destroyers on the screen (temporary boys – H's) never saw them coming until they dropped. We opened a hell of a fire and I saw bits coming off one aircraft as it roared past but I didn't see it crash. Again Mac combed most skilfully but it was the last attack we had.

During the night, one of the MT ships *Empire Song* was mined in the Narrows and blew up after being set on fire. Two mines had exploded in her paravanes, but she was able to steam for four hours before her ammunition stores exploded; her survivors were taken to Malta. *New Zealand Star* was also damaged by a mine but her speed was not affected. Cunningham had sailed with the Mediterranean Fleet to meet the convoy 50 miles south of Malta, bombarding Benghazi on the way. Helped to a large extent by extraordinary thick weather off Malta which prevailed for the rest of the journey, the four surviving MT ships arrived in Alexandria carrying 238 tanks and 43 Hurricanes. Meanwhile Force H remained south of Sardinia to cover the return from Malta of the 8th DF destroyers who had escorted the convoy through the Narrows. *Foresight* was bombed and hit and her speed reduced to 7 knots in the westerly gale. It was an anxious time escorting her, as the ships were within bombing range from Sardinia and *Ark Royal* had only four fighters serviceable. Somerville's staff urged him not to risk his valuable ships for the sake of one destroyer. But he refused to 'leave his little boats unprotected; if Dad does not take a chance to help the Boys, the latter will inevitably lose confidence'. It was this attitude which brought him the devotion of all who served under him. The destroyer's crew 'cheered like mad when they saw the old familiar party heave in sight'.

The weather eased during the night and speed could be increased to 12 knots. All ships returned safely to Gibraltar after an eight-day operation in which the destroyers had been at action stations for seventy-two hours without a break. That there were no hits on the British ships from air attacks on the outward passage was thanks to the intensive AA gunfire of the force and above all to the magnificent performance of the Fulmars. The driving off of a large force of Ju 87s and Me 110s by seven Fulmars was a formidable achievement, and the skilful handling of *Ark Royal* and *Renown* by their Captains was much praised. The Prime Minister's faith in the operation was justified, to his great relief. But Cunningham was concerned that the apparent ease with which a convoy was brought through from end to end of the Mediterranean had caused many false conclusions to be drawn at home, not least that the dangers of the passage had been exaggerated. He was also scornful that the tanks and Hurricanes, having survived the perilous voyage, had had to be stored on arrival for fitting sand and dust filters and were thus open to attack from German aircraft; these filters should have been fitted before the departure from Britain.[10]

Furious arrived at Gibraltar on 18 May. By detaching the wings of the Hurricanes she was able to carry forty-eight of the aircraft in her hangar. The wings were now reattached and twenty-two planes transferred to *Ark Royal*, the remainder retained in *Furious* to fly off. On this and other occasions when *Furious* brought out Hurricanes for a Club Run, some of which were to be transferred to *Ark Royal*, it was the practice for the two ships to be berthed stern to stern and a ramp placed between their flight decks so that the Hurricanes could be wheeled across from one ship to the other. But because this activity could be seen from Algeciras, the transfer had to take place at night.

Both ships sailed next day for a Club Run, escorted by *Renown*, *Sheffield* and six destroyers. On 21 May, forty-eight fighters were flown off, escorted by five Fulmars; one Hurricane failed to arrive. One of the Fulmars after taking off was unable to retract its undercarriage. The pilot wished to return and land on, but the section of Hurricanes he had been due to lead to Malta had firmly attached themselves to him and could not be made to understand that they were to transfer to the relief Fulmar which had taken off. Appreciating that every minute counted if the Hurricanes were to reach Malta before their fuel ran out, rather than waste time and risk the loss of the whole formation the Fulmar crew set off on their journey knowing that with its undercarriage down the plane would almost certainly not have sufficient fuel to complete the journey. The plane did indeed have to ditch, but happily the crew were rescued. One Hurricane failed to arrive. Force H returned to harbour berthing at 2245 on 22 May.

Meanwhile in the eastern basin, the Mediterranean Fleet was facing a harder task. The Tiger convoy had been fought through to support the land campaign along the African shoreline. There was now also a land battle being fought on the northern side of the Sea in which it would become involved. In April Hitler launched a short and savage attack against Yugoslavia and Greece, countries which, unlike Rumania, Hungary and Bulgaria, had not submitted to his demands in the Balkans area. A small British and Dominion force was sent to Greece in early March to forestall the criticism that would have been voiced by neutral opinion, especially in America, if no support had been given. However, with the Luftwaffe exercising air superiority, the forces available could not withstand the drive of the panzer divisions. The German air strength was at its peak at this time, much of the Fliegerkorps X having been transferred from Sicily to the Balkans. Athens was captured in three weeks, and by the end of April the last British forces were evacuated either back to Egypt or to Crete.

The German attack on Crete began on 20 May, shortly after the Tiger convoy had reached Alexandria, and was led by parachutists and glider troops. No seaborne landings were made by the enemy until after his airborne forces had captured the island. Within a week the Royal Navy, with the 1939–40 precedents of Norway and Dunkirk still fresh in the memory, was once again preparing an evacuation of ground troops. About 18,600 of the 32,000 men in the garrison were embarked, most of them reaching Egypt safely. In these operations around Crete two battleships and one aircraft carrier were damaged, three cruisers and six destroyers sunk, and six cruisers and seven destroyers damaged. The effort made by the fleet had been magnificent. As Cunningham said in his despatch, his men had 'started the evacuation already overtired and … had to carry it through under savage air attack. It is perhaps even now not realised how nearly the breaking point was reached. But that these men struggled through is a measure of their achievement.'[11] The Mediterranean Fleet lost more than 2000 men.

The loss of Crete with its airfields and naval base at Suda Bay marked a significant change in naval strategy in the Mediterranean. The Mediterranean Fleet had won two notable victories over the Italian Fleet: on 11 November 1940 in a crushing attack on the Italian battlefleet at Taranto when Swordfish from the *Illustrious* sank three battleships; and four months later off Cape Matapan south of Greece when the fleet sank three cruisers and damaged a battleship. The balance of sea power was changed in this respect, but with the Germans now in control of the north and south sides of the Mediterranean east of Malta and operating a reinforced Luftwaffe, the supply and relief of the island from the west became Force H's main responsibility.

THE *BISMARCK* ACTION

On 23 May the German battleship *Bismarck* – the largest and most menacing in the world – and the cruiser *Prinz Eugen* left their anchorage in Norway. In anticipation of *Bismarck*'s departure, the Commander-in-Chief Home Fleet had strengthened the cruiser patrol lines in the Denmark Strait and in the Iceland–Faeroes gap, and sent the battleships *Hood* and *Prince of Wales* on ahead to refuel at Hvalfjord in Iceland. Tovey now sailed from Scapa in *King George V* with the new carrier *Victorious* and four cruisers, and was joined next day by the battlecruiser *Repulse* sailing from Greenock. The Admiralty diverted *Rodney* on passage to the United States for a refit; ordered the battleships *Revenge* to leave Halifax and *Ramillies* to leave her convoy; and Force H, just returned to

Gibraltar from a Club Run, to sail into the Atlantic to escort a southbound troop convoy WS 8B. Overall, therefore, there was an initial deployment of eight capital ships and two aircraft carriers to counter the lethal threat to Atlantic shipping represented by *Bismarck*. Force H sailed at 0200 on 24 May.

Bismarck was detected north of Iceland near the ice belt by two cruisers, who did admirable and classical shadowing in very difficult conditions. *Hood* and *Prince of Wales* made contact. *Hood* was hit and blew up and *Prince of Wales* was damaged in the engagement that followed. The loss of the *Hood* was a shock – to those in the Navy a very great shock. Her limitations were well known: she was an old ship with limited deck armour and had not had a proper modernisation. But she was the 'mighty *Hood*', a fine-looking and majestic ship, the pride of the Navy, with immense prestige and a worldwide reputation. Her loss was keenly felt and there was a deep sense of depression throughout *Ark Royal*. When Tovey was within 100 miles of *Bismarck*, he detached *Victorious* with the cruisers to launch a torpedo strike. The *Victorious* was newly commissioned and had been preparing for a Club Run from Gibraltar, and her hangar was half full of crated fighters. She had just embarked No. 825 Squadron of nine Swordfish which was still being worked up to full efficiency and this was their first trip in the ship. A strike was launched and two hits claimed. Two of the shadowing Fulmars were lost.

Contact was then lost with the *Bismarck*, and the next thirty-one hours were a very anxious period. Had she continued into the Atlantic to rendezvous with a supply ship, or returned to Germany, or was she making for Brest? It had been reported that she was leaking oil after the action in the Denmark Strait and there were repair facilities in Brest and a large dry dock at St Nazaire. The Commander-in-Chief decided that this was the more likely course and made his dispositions – confirmed shortly afterwards by Enigma decoding of *Bismarck*'s transmissions. Force H was ordered north to intercept. The increasingly bad weather caused speed to be reduced progressively through the night from 25 to 17 knots; *Renown* and *Sheffield* were 'taking it green' over the superstructure and *Ark Royal*'s flight deck was out of bounds. The destroyers were ordered to return to Gibraltar on the morning of 25 May, spread to twice visibility distance in daylight in case the battlecruisers *Gneisenau* and *Scharnhorst* had left Brest during the night. It was an especially anxious time for Somerville. His ships were the only force between *Bismarck* and Brest, and if the battlecruisers came out to support *Bismarck* they would be an overwhelming force against him. It was a very tense time for everyone involved, both ashore and afloat. Even though the destination was known the detection of a ship in the poor weather conditions of the Atlantic was highly uncertain, and an additional worry was that ships were getting short of fuel after so much high-speed steaming. There was the grim realisation that if she was not found and brought to action, the Royal Navy would have been defeated by the German Navy.

At last on the morning of 26 May a Catalina sighted *Bismarck* 700 miles from Brest and 112 miles north-west of Force H. *Ark Royal* sent up her recce planes to confirm the position and hold on to her. The *Prinz Eugen* had a very similar silhouette and to make sure it was *Bismarck* Somerville ordered up Swordfish fitted with long-range tanks and experienced ship-recognition observers. This sortie in an open cockpit in that Atlantic weather, and subsequent five-hour shadowing sorties, cannot have been pleasant. To make sure that contact would not be lost again, Somerville sent *Sheffield* on ahead to shadow the enemy ship. It was evident at this time that unless the enemy's speed could be reduced, the Commander-in-Chief would not be able to catch up and it was doubtful whether his battleships would have enough fuel to continue the chase another day. Everything now depended on Force H. This was the last chance to stop the *Bismarck*.

The weather was really foul. It was blowing hard from the north-west and the ships were punching into a filthy sea. *Ark Royal*'s rounddown (the rear end of her flight deck) was rising and falling 56 feet. Aircraft could slide sideways across the wet deck and had to be double lashed. The conditions for operating aircraft came into the category described in the handbook as 'extremely severe and entailing a great hazard to aircraft'.[12] The Swordfish, already a museum piece that had to be manually started, was probably the only carrier plane in the world that could have mastered these conditions. There was a vicious circle here – the Swordfish stalling speed was 55 knots and, with a gale-force wind of 40 knots along the deck, the carrier had to slow down to 8 or 10 knots, otherwise the planes would have blown back off the stern on landing; and it was this slow ship's speed which caused the ship to pitch so heavily. And it was now that Somerville's close interest in flying operations paid off. The aircrew knew that their Admiral had a proper appreciation of what he was asking them to do, and they respected his judgement.

Force H had crossed ahead of the *Bismarck* so as to keep to windward both to avoid *Ark Royal* closing the enemy when altering to a north-westerly course for operating aircraft and to allow for the enemy making a substantial detour to the south, while maintaining an intercepting position to the eastward throughout – holding the 'weather gauge' (see Glossary) yet again proving to be of significance in this most modern of sea battles. Once the flying on or off of the aircraft had been completed, speed was increased to 29 knots downwind to recover lost ground. The objective was to launch a torpedo attack that would reduce *Bismarck*'s speed and allow Tovey in *King George V*, with *Rodney* now in company, to catch her. They were 130 miles behind to the west steaming as fast as *Rodney*'s leaky boiler tubes permitted, which was only 22 knots. There was a suggestion that a squadron of Fulmars might make dummy dive-bombing attacks as a diversion, but these heavier planes required a longer take off and landing approach than the weather conditions would permit.

At 1515 fifteen Swordfish from 810 and 820 Squadrons took off from the heaving and pitching deck. Because of the bad weather the planes were relying on an ASV set carried on one of the Swordfish, which located a ship 20 miles from the position previously given to the leader. The aircraft duly attacked this ship, but it was the wrong target. They returned two hours later to report that in the thick weather they had attacked *Sheffield* by mistake. What had happened was that the signal detaching *Sheffield* had not been repeated to *Ark Royal*; her presence was not known to the aircrews and in the very poor visibility it was assumed she was the enemy. The first sub-flight realised the mistake and fired off red Very lights to warn the following planes. But some of the other pilots, all hyped up for the attack, mistook the flares for enemy flak and pressed on with their attack.[13] *Sheffield* increased to full speed and took avoiding action of the eleven torpedoes dropped, and there were no hits. Two torpedoes fitted with duplex pistols in their warhead were seen to detonate on impact with the water and three more exploded when crossing *Sheffield*'s wake. A fortuitous outcome from this wasted attack was that it demonstrated the unsuitability of magnetic pistols in the prevailing sea conditions. Three of the aircraft were damaged on landing.

As soon as the crews were rested and the aircraft refuelled and rearmed, fifteen aircraft – representing all the serviceable Swordfish available – took off again, still in atrocious weather, this time with contact pistols fitted and torpedoes set to run at a depth of 22 feet. The Swordfish profile for attack is to make the final approach, which must be steady, at 100 knots or best speed and 60–100 feet, dropping torpedo at 1000 yards or less from the target. The *Bismarck* put up heavy AA fire, which included firing her 15-inch guns in a flat trajectory to cause water splashes 100 feet high through which the aircraft had to fly. The determination of the pilots in carrying out such a close-range attack in their vulnerable, slow and elderly planes merits a full description, and this is taken from Somerville's official report of the action:[14]

The striking force had orders to make contact with *Sheffield* before launching the attack, both to ensure gaining contact with the enemy and to avoid any possibility of *Sheffield* being mistaken for the target. *Sheffield* was instructed to home the striking force by D/F.

The aircraft approached *Sheffield* at 1955 below the clouds and then climbed to a height of 6000 feet. The weather conditions at this time appeared to be ideal for a synchronised torpedo attack, cloud 7/10 from 2000 to 5000 feet. During the climb contact was lost with *Sheffield* but regained at 2035 when a bearing and distance (110º, 12 miles) of *Bismarck* was passed by *Sheffield* by V/S. The force took departure for the target in sub-flights in line astern at 2040. On nearing the enemy a thick bank of cloud with base about 700 feet and top between 6000 and 10,000 feet was encountered and the force split up. At 2047, when it was calculated that the enemy would be in a suitable position for an attack down wind from astern, No.1 sub-flight dived down through the cloud, but on reaching the base the enemy was seen down wind to the eastward. Position for an attack on the port beam was gained by approaching just in the clouds, and the final dive to attack was made at 2055. One aircraft from No.3 sub-flight followed closely and also attacked from the port beam. This aircraft observed a hit on *Bismarck* about two-thirds of her length from forward. All four aircraft came under intense and accurate fire from the first moment of sighting until out of range.

Somerville went on to describe the actions of the other Swordfish:

No.2 sub-flight, having climbed to 9000 feet, dived down on a bearing obtained by ASV radar and two aircraft attacked from the starboard beam under intense fire. The third aircraft having lost touch with his sub-flight in the clouds returned to *Sheffield* for a range and bearing on the target. Having obtained this he pressed home a lone and determined attack from the port bow in face of very heavy opposition, and his crew saw the torpedo strike *Bismarck* amidships port side.

No. 4 sub-flight followed No. 3 sub-flight into the cloud and became iced up at 6000 feet. After 7 minutes the aircraft dived and found a clear patch at 2000 feet. *Bismarck* was sighted almost at once engaging No. 2 sub-flight to starboard. All four aircraft circled astern of the target and attacked simultaneously from port coming under heavy fire. One aircraft was hit many times and both pilot and air gunner were wounded, the observer being uninjured. 175 holes were counted in this aircraft which had to be written off as one of the longerons had been cut.

No. 5 sub-flight of two aircraft lost contact with the remainder and with each other in the cloud. Having started to ice up at 7000 feet they came down and while still in cloud at 3500 feet one was engaged by AA fire. On coming out of the cloud the pilot saw the enemy ahead of him and down wind so retired into the cloud, being engaged continuously while gaining a more favourable position. He eventually came in low on the *Bismarck*'s starboard bow and dropped just outside 1000 yards. The other aircraft of this sub-flight made three attempts to come in but was so heavily engaged on each appearance that he finally jettisoned his torpedo and returned to *Ark Royal*.

No. 6 sub-flight followed into the cloud and when at 6300 feet turned 40° to port and climbed clear at 7450 feet, waited for about 15 minutes and returned to *Sheffield* for another range and bearing of the enemy. These two aircraft then searched at sea level and attacked on the starboard beam. Intense fire prevented close approach and one dropped at about 4000 yards while the other returned to the carrier and jettisoned before landing on.

The striking force attack took much longer than had been anticipated (2055 to 2125) owing to bad weather conditions around *Bismarck* who appeared to be under a cold front.

The actual attack was described by Sub Lieutenant G. A. Woods RNVR, Observer in No. 4 sub-flight, in his book *Wings at Sea*:[15]

The minute or so which followed will be forever engraved on my memory. There she was, a thousand yards away, big, black, cowled funnel, menacing, with every close range weapon stabbing flame as we steadied on our approach, 100 knots, 100 feet, 1000 yards just as the text book says. 'Flash' Seager, the TAG, was sensibly crouching down in the cockpit, sitting on a lead-covered codebook. Later he told me I was shouting my head off as we ran in, probably true, but what it was I have no idea. All I know is that as we dropped our 'tinfish', 'A4Charlie' [aircraft in No. 4 sub-flight] almost leapt in the air, and as we turned away aft tightly, we were suspended motionless for a split second that felt like an eternity as every gun seemed to concentrate upon us. The flak ripped through the fabric-covered fuselage like peas on a drum. 'Flash' yelled, and then Alan [Swanton, the pilot] said 'Christ! Just look at this lot' as *Bismarck* put her 15-inch guns on a flat trajectory, firing ahead of us, either intending to blast us off the face of the earth, or as happened in fact, to make a Beecher's Brook of water splashes 100 feet high through which we must fly, and which might bring us spinning down into the raging sea. 'Flash's normally sallow complexion looked grey, but at that time it didn't worry me, because I had no idea what colour I was, probable even more grey than he.

But they did not escape unscathed:

As we sped aft, opening the range, and out of immediate danger, I asked him if he was all right, and he said yes, but did not look at all happy, and went on to say he had been hit in the buttocks, so I turned and spoke to Alan, telling him this and giving him a course back to the ship. I saw Alan's overalls were torn in the right shoulder and asked if he was all right. He said yes, but there was blood seeping down his back 'How long before we're there?' he asked, 'about 25 minutes', 'OK, I can hold on'. That was about the sum of our conversation. I had escaped injury but the burst which must have wounded them both had gone clean through my Mae West life jacket near the left shoulder, and the kapok was welling out. At first I thought they were my tripes, but realised they weren't up there.

Meanwhile we had formated on 'Scruffy' Manley-Cooper with his beloved radar set, and on the other side was Jock Moffat, as usual laughing his head off. And so we came back. During the trip the other two aircraft had been warned that I was going to request an emergency landing priority, and they went away to allow me to fire red Very lights and signal with the Aldis lamp. Quickly *Ark* acknowledged the fact that pilot and air gunner were wounded and cleared the deck for what might have been a very ropey landing. But all was well, Alan held her off until the last moment and she sank lightly on to the deck. Straight up and through the lowered barrier we went and stretchers came alongside for the wounded. Alan was able to walk to the sickbay. But poor Seager, in great pain, had to be carried.

No Swordfish were lost. Two planes suffered damaged undercarriages on landing and Woods' aircraft in No. 4 sub-flight, which had received so much damage, was a write-off. The Swordfish obtained two hits, one torpedo hitting *Bismarck*'s steering-gear compartment. The ship made two complete circles and never seemed to be under full control again. During one of these turns *Sheffield*, who had been shadowing from astern, suddenly found *Bismarck* steering straight for her. The battleship fired six accurate 15-inch salvoes at the cruiser at a range of 9 miles, causing casualties of one killed, two later dying of their wounds, and eight wounded. Some splinter damage was sustained, affecting radar performance.

It then became too dark for a third sortie to be flown off from *Ark Royal*, but during the night *Cossack* and three other destroyers under Captain Philip Vian carried out torpedo attacks and claimed two hits. The destroyers fired starshell every half-hour to indicate the position of the enemy, whose speed had been reduced to 8 knots. The Commander-in-Chief ordered Force H to move to the south of *Bismarck* while he kept to the north. At this stage, *Renown* and *Ark Royal*, who were without any destroyer screen, were sighted by and passed close to U-boat 556 returning from an Atlantic patrol – which fortunately had expended all its torpedoes. Somerville's guardian angel was still co-operating.

Next morning Somerville was in considerable doubt about the position of *King George V* and *Rodney*. Earlier he had received explicit instructions from the Admiralty that *Renown* was not to engage *Bismarck* unless *King George V* and *Rodney* were already fully engaged. Because of the low visibility he considered it imperative to afford *Ark Royal* the maximum protection should *King George V* fail to establish contact, so *Renown* remained with *Ark Royal*. The weather was still horrible and *Ark Royal* had to strike down her aircraft as it was impossible to keep them ranged on deck. Nevertheless at 0926 twelve Swordfish were flown off. The sound of gunfire was heard, indicating that the Commander-in-Chief was finally in action. *Bismarck* was now being battered by the 14-inch and 16-inch guns of *King George V* and *Rodney*. At last, ending one of the most momentous engagements of the war, the stricken battleship was sunk, hit by torpedoes from the cruiser *Dorsetshire*. The Swordfish were recalled and had to ditch their torpedoes as it was too dangerous to land on the ship with them in that weather. Now that they were within bomber range of the French coast the ships came under air attack and one Home Fleet destroyer was sunk. A Heinkel dropped a stick of bombs while *Ark Royal* was landing on her planes, which just missed astern of her.

Force H steamed south at 24 knots and returned to a rousing welcome at Gibraltar, *Ark Royal* leading the way into harbour ahead of *Renown*. The loss of the *Hood* had been avenged and the Navy had been spared the ignominy and embarrassment of being defeated at sea in battle. If *Bismarck* had reached Brest, the German victory – sinking the *Hood*, Britain's largest battleship, and driving off the *Prince of Wales*, its newest battleship – would have been triumphantly proclaimed. Confidence overseas in Britain's ability to withstand

Germany would have been weakened, including in America (not yet in the war), where the 3000-mile chase had excited much attention. And with *Bismarck*, *Gneisenau* and *Scharnhorst*, to be joined shortly by *Prinz Eugen*, all at Brest, the threat of such a formidable force to Atlantic shipping needed no stressing. The *Bismarck* had to be stopped and sunk. It was a close-run thing, but Force H made it happen.

The euphoria at Gibraltar lasted several days. Churchill sent his congratulations. The BBC lauded the aircrews. Swordfish crews had their pictures taken, and were interviewed by Gaumont British News for a news-hungry British public. On 30 May all Swordfish crews were summoned onboard *Renown* to be presented to the Governor, Lord Gort, and for more interviews. Somerville, as was his wont, sought out a quiet corner where he could converse with the sub-lieutenants and midshipmen of the Air Branch, 'to find out', as he put it, 'what *really* happened'. At the celebration dinner the main dish on the menu could only be 'Swordfish Suprême'.

FORCE H: ONE YEAR IN BEING

It was about this time that Somerville decided that the manner in which the Club Runs were being conducted was now definitely compromised. The enemy was likely to take special steps to obtain early information about the arrival of Hurricanes at Gibraltar. On learning of Force H's departure it could be expected to concentrate submarine, surface and air attacks about 6° East before the planes were flown off; and fighters could be positioned to engage the Hurricanes while on passage and heavy attacks made on Malta while they were landing. To defeat these moves and to exploit the use of the Hurricanes when fitted with auxiliary tanks, allowing a further flying distance of 100–150 miles, for the next operation he proposed to fly them off in two flights, each of twenty-two aircraft, about 600 miles from Malta, to which they would be escorted by Catalinas. This radical new arrangement would take the enemy by surprise and give Force H more flexibility in the times it sailed from Gibraltar. A Catalina used as escort had greater reliability and endurance than the Hurricanes being escorted, whereas the reverse was true of a Fulmar used as escort. But the Air Ministry vetoed the employment of Catalinas, and instead it was Blenheims and Hudsons, although they had a lesser reserve of endurance, that took part in the forthcoming Club Runs.

Argus arrived at Gibraltar at midnight on 30 May and berthed astern of *Furious*, so that her cargo of Hurricanes could be transferred by ramp between the two flight decks. She sailed at 0445 to be clear of the harbour before dawn. *Ark Royal* embarked three Sea Hurricanes for the first time as part of her complement. With *Furious* in company Force H sailed for a Club Run on 5 June. Forty-four Hurricanes were flown off in four flights, each led by two Blenheims. One Hurricane returned to *Furious* with undercarriage down, indicating that an emergency landing was required. After allowing seven minutes for the ship to work up to full speed, the aircraft touched deck on the first attempt to land but was going too fast and, showing good judgement, took off again. The pilot then made an excellent landing on the second attempt, when the wind speed over the deck was 36 knots. The remaining aircraft arrived safely at Malta. While the Blenheim was considered a more suitable aircraft than a Fulmar for escorting the fighters, its inability to communicate easily by V/S because of the restricted arc available in the cockpit limited its effectiveness.

A repeat performance was carried out on 13 June, on this occasion *Victorious* making her first Club Run after transferring Hurricanes by ramp in a similar way. Forty-seven Hurricanes were flown off escorted by four Hudsons. All arrived safely except one that crashed into the sea and another that was seen to break formation and make for the African coast. A further series of operations on 26–29 June entailed *Ark Royal* and *Furious* flying off forty fighters. There was a mishap in *Furious* when, on taking off, the second Hurricane swerved and hit the bridge structure. The aircraft went over the side, but not before flaming petrol enveloped the bridge and surrounds. With the bridge burning furiously, the ship was turned out of the wind and the engines stopped. Flying was not resumed until the fire was under control. 820 Squadron, on completion of its very distinguished service in *Ark Royal*, returned to UK in *Victorious* and was relieved by 825 Squadron.

Other events in June included Force H sailing into the Atlantic on 7 June to avoid being caught in harbour in anticipation of a retaliatory bombing attack by French aircraft prompted by forthcoming Allied operations in Syria, but no attack materialised. On 18 June five destroyers of the 8th DF, returning to Gibraltar after escorting *Victorious* homebound for Britain, sank a German U-boat in the Atlantic. Its survivors were shocked to see *Ark Royal* in harbour, given that German propaganda had assured them many times that she had been sunk. The destroyers sailed again on 22 June to intercept an enemy supply ship or raider reported in the Atlantic. The ship, *Alstertor*, signalled that she had prisoners on board but scuttled herself before she could be boarded. The survivors picked up included British and German personnel. Two destroyers *Lance* and *Lively* were loaned to Force H from the Home Fleet to replace *Fearless* and *Foxhound*, who were suffering defects after hard running. *Hermione*, who had now relieved

Sheffield and was fitted with a more powerful radar, joined the force for the Club Runs on 26 and 28 June. All aircraft arrived at Malta, but one crashed on landing.

On 28 June Force H celebrated its first birthday. After its difficult first six months, the performance of the force had been impressive. In the Mediterranean it had taken the offensive to the Italian mainland with the bombardment of Genoa, achieving complete surprise. The Club Runs had become a familiar, almost routine, event, and the number of Hurricanes successfully flown off and through to Malta had been greatly increased. Although the island's fighter strength had been increased fivefold since January by these reinforcements, thirty-two had been lost in combat and nearly as many destroyed on the ground. Between April and June, 214 Hurricanes had been flown through to Malta, half of which went on to join the Desert Air Force. And despite the severity of the air attacks resulting from the Luftwaffe's deployment, the passage of the two military convoys comprising nine MT ships was achieved with, surprisingly, the loss of only one ship.

In the Atlantic there were the essential, but unreported, long dull periods of patrolling or escorting convoys, typical of warfare in that ocean. The Admiralty regarded the Battle of the Atlantic as of supreme importance, over all other commitments, and the 'two ocean' nature of Force H was evident in the amount of time the force spent in the Atlantic in these first months of 1941. There were the emergency sailings from Gibraltar on receiving sighting reports of German warships, generally at high speeds; or the patrolling off Brest in conjunction with the Home Fleet; or the escorting of convoys, either the fast WS troop convoys of 15 knots or slow 7-knot convoys – such low speeds always anathema to Somerville. The amount of sea time was impressive. At one stage Force H returned to Gibraltar having been at sea for fifty days out of the preceding fifty-six, only to go to sea again for another fourteen days' patrol. This record of sea time was probably not equalled by any other fleet during the war.[16] The disappointment the force felt at having missed making contact with the *Gneisenau* and *Scharnhorst* before they reached Brest was more than compensated for by the key role it played in the sinking of the *Bismarck*. In that action the flexibility of maritime power was demonstrated. The invaluable role of the aircraft carrier was never better evidenced than by *Ark Royal*'s performance in flying off twenty-two Hurricanes to Malta well inside the Mediterranean on 21 May and in crippling *Bismarck* with her Swordfish torpedo bombers some 450 miles west of Brest six days later.[17] This was Force H's proudest hour. It was not known at the time, but the action marked the final defeat of the enemy's attempts to disrupt Atlantic shipping with his surface forces.[18]

Somerville had also developed a more cordial relationship with the Admiralty. However, his application to be restored to the Active List was unsuccessful. Just before sailing for the *Bismarck* action he was told that 'Their Lordships were loath to refuse his request but regretted they must adhere to established precedent.'[19] One may speculate whether the same reply would have been given a week later. In fact in financial terms the Admiralty's decision benefited him: as an invalided vice admiral recalled for service he was better off than he would have been as a vice admiral restored to the Active List.

The first year of Force H closed on a sombre note with the German invasion of Russia on 21 June. Victory seemed a long way off.

AT FULL STRETCH

WITH THE **G**ERMANS now in control of Crete and Greece and dominating the north side of the eastern Mediterranean, and with their troops in occupation of the African coast along the south side, naval operations in the eastern Mediterranean were much more hazardous. Malta had to rely on supply from the west. The ferrying of Hurricanes to be flown off for its fighter defence was kept up and relief convoys to take supplies to the beleaguered island were inaugurated. Hitherto only a few merchant ships carrying military equipment had been escorted, but convoys on a larger scale were now needed, requiring a massive supporting force. The passage of a convoy became a major fleet operation. There were to be four such convoys during the next year, the first two taking place in the coming three months. Fortunately, withdrawal of much of the Luftwaffe to the Russian front eased the scale of air attack for the next few months.

MALTA CONVOY – JULY 1941

The convoy of July 1941, codeword Substance, was the first major Malta convoy to bring relief to the island. It consisted of seven transports containing personnel and stores, with additional escort provided by the Home Fleet of one battleship, *Nelson*, three cruisers *Edinburgh*, *Manchester* and *Arethusa*, eight destroyers and the fast minelayer *Manxman*. The operation would also entail taking seven merchant ships who had discharged their cargo at Malta back to Gibraltar. Troops for the passage to Malta had been brought out in the French liner *Pasteur* and were transferred to *Manchester* and *Arethusa* at Gibraltar. The convoy passed through the Straits at night in fog. The troop-carrying *Leinster*, with RAF personnel onboard joining from Gibraltar, ran aground and took no further part in the operation. Force H, forming up with the convoy and its escort from the Home Fleet on 21 July, consisted of *Renown*, *Ark Royal*, *Hermione* and eight destroyers. Somerville was in command of the whole operation.

On Day 3, the customary day for the first air attack, a well-synchronised torpedo and high-level bombing attack achieved hits on *Fearless* and *Manchester*. *Fearless* took avoiding action and the first torpedo passed 90 yards ahead, and the ship was stemming the course of the second torpedo when it broke surface, altered course and hit her. There were large explosions and the destroyer was soon badly on fire, with engines disabled; one officer and thirty-four ratings were killed. The crew had to be taken off and the ship sunk. *Fearless* was the first of the F class destroyers of Force H to be lost. In the attack on *Manchester* two torpedoes passed down the port side and one astern to starboard when the tracks were combed. But course had to be altered to avoid collision with *Port Chalmers* and another torpedo struck her on the port side aft. She was severely damaged with thirty-five killed and nine wounded but could still make 9 knots. There were 750 troops onboard, and Somerville ordered her to return to Gibraltar, escorted by *Avon Vale*. Only the starboard outer shaft remained available and her speed was limited to 8 knots, but was gradually increased to 12 knots. She was attacked later by three torpedo bombers which approached from up-sun, having proceeded well into territorial waters to reach that position. AA fire was effective and the ship was not hit. Later in the day there was a further air attack on the convoy but the enemy formation was broken up and the attack was abortive. Enemy losses were two high-level bombers shot down by Fulmars, three torpedo bombers by gunfire in the first attack of the day, and two torpedo bombers by Fulmars in the second attack. On reaching the entrance to the Skerki Channel, Force H withdrew to the west to cover *Manchester* but retained a section of fighters over the convoy until 1830, when they were relieved by Beaufighters from Malta.

The escort continuing through to Malta with the convoy was commanded by Rear Admiral E. N. Syfret in *Edinburgh*, who had with him *Arethusa*, *Hermione* (replacing *Manchester*), *Manxman* and ten destroyers. For passage through the Narrows, described in *The Times* as 'the Jaws of Death' but known more aptly to the sailors as 'Bomb Alley', the convoy was in two columns, each led by a destroyer with TSDS minesweeping equipment streamed. The escorts were closely stationed around the merchant ships. At 1900 four torpedo bombers attacked, but avoiding action by ships was successful and one plane was shot down. A high-level bombing raid shortly afterwards was not

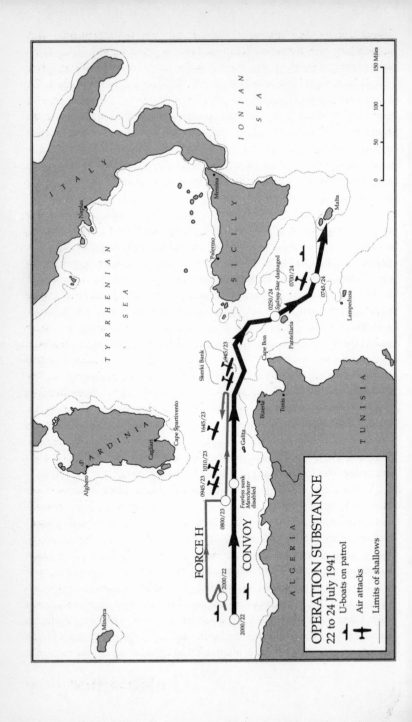

OPERATION SUBSTANCE
22 to 24 July 1941

FORCE H

CONVOY

✈ U-boats on patrol
✈ Air attacks
— Limits of shallows

ITALY

Naples

TYRRHENIAN
SEA

SARDINIA

Cagliari

Alghero

Minorca

Cape Spartivento

Palermo

Messina

SICILY

Skerki Bank

Cape Bon

Pantelleria

Bizerta

Tunis

Galita

TUNISIA

ALGERIA

IONIAN
SEA

Malta

Lampedusa

0745/24

0700/24

0250/24 Sydney Star damaged

1945/23

1645/23

1010/23

0945/23

0800/23

Fearless sunk
Manchester disabled

2000/22

2000/22

0   50   100   150 Miles

intercepted by Beaufighters, who failed to carry out instructions and, approaching from the same direction as the enemy without identifying themselves, were engaged by the gunfire of the fleet. In the bombing attack *Firedrake*, towing TSDS ahead of the port column, was holed in the boiler room, and *Eridge* took her in tow to return to Gibraltar. *Firedrake*'s steering gear was out of action and she had considerable difficulty in turning to the course for the Galita Channel. After being in tow for thirty-nine hours she was able to proceed under her own power and make 9 knots. Syfret decided to accept the increased risk of damage by mines and not replace her; the screen was already materially reduced and the delay in streaming a sweep could not be accepted.

At 0250 that night, when the convoy was nearing Pantellaria, the sound of engines being started up indicated the presence of E-boats. In the ensuing mêlée under searchlight illumination and much close-range gunfire from pom-poms and Oerlikons, the E-boats fired torpedoes. Ships' gunfire damaged four boats, but one British merchant ship, *Sydney Star*, was hit and took in 30 feet of water in the hold. She appeared to be sinking and *Nestor* closed to take off the 470 troops she was carrying; the transfer took fifty minutes, with the ships stopped 4 miles from Pantellaria. While alongside, *Nestor* gained the impression that the ship could be kept afloat and urged her Master to get under way again. She was able to steam at 12 knots. *Nestor* and *Sydney Star* drove off two torpedo-bomber attacks in the morning and were joined by *Hermione* to give additional AA protection. By this time *Nestor* had 774 people onboard (231 ship's company, 56 army passengers, 487 ex-*Sydney Star*). A further attack on this small force came from Ju 87 dive bombers and two high-level bombers; it was well synchronised but no ship was hit, and one Ju 87 was shot down. All ships of the convoy and escort arrived at Malta without further incident, delivering some 65,000 tons of cargo.

Meanwhile Force H was covering several ship formations. *Manchester* and *Avon Vale* were 60 miles to the westward proceeding at 11 knots towards Gibraltar; south of Galita, an island lying to the north of the Tunisian coastline, *Firedrake* and *Eridge* were making 8 knots; and in a 60-mile strip also in the Galita area were three groups of empty merchant ships sailing from Malta to Gibraltar. Bombers or torpedo bombers attacked all three groups but none was hit. Force H continued westward until 1330 when *Manchester* was reasonably clear of air attacks and would have been met by two destroyers sent from Gibraltar to escort her. Course was then reversed to the east in order to fly off six Swordfish for Malta during the night, and to rendezvous with the convoy escort returning from Malta off Galita Island in the morning. All

Swordfish arrived safely at Malta. At 1035 on 25 July, the combined force was approached by a large group of aircraft. The Fulmars attacked the formation with great dash and caused many bombs to be jettisoned. Three or four bombers were shot down and two damaged, for the loss of two Fulmars; the crew of one was recovered unhurt. *Manchester* arrived at Gibraltar early on 26 July and Force H one day later. On the way back Somerville manoeuvred the fleet to pass close to *Firedrake*, now escorted by *Eridge* and *Avon Vale*, on opposite courses to 'cheer ship'. The hole in *Firedrake*'s side was large enough to allow Somerville to row into the boiler room in his skiff on one of his morning exercise tours of the harbour.

Throughout the convoy operation *Ark Royal*'s Fulmars contributed much to the safe arrival of the convoy at its destination. Six Fulmars were lost, with the crews of four being picked up unhurt. No merchant ship in the convoy or of those returning empty was sunk, but the escort lost one destroyer sunk, and one cruiser and one destroyer damaged. Somerville was concerned that the Italians should manage two torpedo hits in a day attack, but the success of the operation was a remarkable achievement, even given that most of the German aircraft had been withdrawn from Sicily. Somerville confessed that he had never expected to get all merchant ships through or, even more miraculous, to get the seven empty ships back. A significant factor in the success was no doubt his insistence on the high standards he set for the Substance convoy, which have been noted earlier (see p. 17–18 above). The press made much of the success of the operation. 'THE CONVOY MUST GO THROUGH' provided banner headlines. Signals of congratulations poured in, including a personal message from Churchill. The First Lord of the Admiralty broadcast a message over the BBC lauding the work of Force H, and thus the name Force H finally achieved full public recognition (see Preface above). Somerville was especially pleased that Churchill's message included the words, 'This is only the latest of a long series of complicated and highly successful operations for which you and Force H have been responsible.'

SPECIAL OPERATION

Force H sailed again on 30 July to pass through to Malta the troops who had missed their passage due to *Leinster* grounding and *Manchester* having to turn back. Seventy officers and 1676 ranks were embarked in the cruisers *Hermione* and *Arethusa*, two destroyers and *Manxman*, forming Force X. As a diversion to draw Italian forces north and give Force X a clear run to Malta, *Ark Royal* flew off nine Swordfish to attack the Alghero aerodrome in Sardinia, and two destroyers shelled the seaplane base. Hits were obtained on the equipment shop, hangars and living quarters. There was a second attack at night. When the aircraft returned after the raid, a 40-pound bomb on the third Swordfish to land, which had not been released clear of the rack, came away and exploded, killing four officers and two ratings and making a 2-foot hole in the deck. The plane became a blazing furnace and it took an hour to get the deck ready for the remaining aircraft, which were circling the ship and rapidly running out of petrol. It was an anxious time, but they all landed safely. On passage *Hermione* rammed and sank an Italian submarine sighted on the surface close on the port bow. The ships arrived unharmed at Malta at 0900 on 2 August and sailed again at 1600. *Farndale*, who had remained at Malta with condenser trouble after the Substance convoy, accompanied the force but could not maintain a speed higher than 18 knots and had to return to Malta. Force X proceeded at 26 knots, passing through Tunisian territorial waters. In both operations after making passage to Malta the ships entered Grand Harbour with ships' companies fallen in, bands playing and troops paraded. The people of Malta gave them a stirring reception. There was no opposition from the Italians for this second operation.

It was now that wear and tear from the high-speed steaming in both the Atlantic and the Mediterranean began to affect the operational capability of Force H. Since joining the force *Renown* had steamed 74,164 miles with 232 days at sea, *Ark Royal* 83,780 miles in 230 days and *Sheffield* over 75,000 miles with 240 days at sea. The 8th DF destroyers had covered an aggregate of 500,000 miles, *Faulknor* steaming 84,000 miles with 266 days at sea. The destroyers were the hardest-run ships of the force, as their time in harbour was often reduced to carry out duties and missions for which the bigger ships were not suited or appropriate. They were also used to supplement the local 13th DF when this was necessary. Somerville declared that the manner in which these little ships kept running reflected the greatest credit on their engine-room departments. After the Substance convoy only three of the Fs were operational (they were starting to be relieved by the L class) and the force could not go to sea except with an entirely inadequate screen. Somerville remarked, 'As for the 8th DF! – I hardly dare look at the poor little sods in the hawse pipes. Run right off their poor little legs and [we] shall end up one day with the whole lot in tow.' Only on rare occasions could the 13th DF provide a fleet destroyer, owing to intense enemy U-boat activity in the area. To make good this deficiency, two Home Fleet destroyers, *Encounter* and *Nestor*, were retained temporarily at Gibraltar. *Renown* was also handicapped. During the last repeat operation to Malta, the port bulge in her hull tore off and folded back, reducing her speed to 18 knots (it had been the starboard bulge that was damaged the previous Christmas). After temporary repairs she sailed for the UK to refit on 8 August, escorted by four of the Home Fleet destroyers which had taken part in the Substance convoy operation. *Nelson* became the new flagship.

Manxman had been part of the escort for the Substance convoy. She was designed as a minelayer capable of very high speeds. With no mines embarked she had a large carrying capacity and was therefore of immense value in taking stores and supplies to Malta. Somerville now planned a bold operation for her off Italy's important northern bases in her prime role. The idea was that the ship, carrying a mixed outfit of mines, would arrive at Gibraltar after dark, refuel and sail before dawn towards the Balearics. The following day at sunset she would increase speed to 37 knots and lay mines off Leghorn in the Gulf of Genoa, returning by the same route and reducing speed for the last day's steaming to Gibraltar. She would arrive there again after dark, refuel and sail for England before dawn. She was to be disguised as a French light cruiser, hoisting the Tricolour on leaving Gibraltar, with the crew in French uniforms during the approach and return from the enemy coast, but casting off disguise when laying the mines. The operation was one of the few occasions during the war when a fast minelayer was to be used in the role for which she had been designed.

To cover the operation *Nelson*, *Ark Royal*, *Hermione* and five destroyers sailed on 20 August. Somerville planned to carry out an incendiary attack on the cork woods at the north end of Sardinia with the aim of implying that this was a front to cover another Malta convoy, thus persuading the Italians to concentrate all their surface forces to the south of Sardinia. As further deception a number of soldiers with full equipment embarked in Force H ships the day before sailing, a piece of play-acting which it was intended should be seen and reported. The ruse worked, and Rome was informed that military reinforcements were being run through to Malta. Iachino and the Italian Fleet sailed to intercept the 'inferior' British force south of Sardinia. The minelaying operation was entirely successful and the air attack set the woods and a factory alight. Sighting reports of the Italian Fleet south of Cagliari were received in the afternoon, consisting of three battleships, six cruisers and twenty-five destroyers. Next day the Italians were again present south of Sardinia, in the belief that the British aim was to pass a convoy through to Malta. They remained within their own fighter cover. However, Force H destroyers had only enough fuel for a few hours of high-speed steaming, so no action could be joined. Returning to Gibraltar the force passed 6 miles off Valencia with fifteen Fulmars and ten Swordfish cruising overhead. This was intended to counter Spanish belief in Italian propaganda that Force H was no longer active. It was reported later that the demonstration was highly effective, the Spanish seeming to be both impressed and pleased by the appearance of the force and the naval aircraft off their waters.[1]

At the end of August Somerville flew home with Lord Gort for talks, which included preparations for the next major convoy to Malta in September. On his return two further Club Runs took place. After dark on 7 September *Furious* was warped close up to *Ark Royal* and twenty-six Hurricanes and one Swordfish were transferred across by ramp. *Ark Royal* and four destroyers sailed next morning; all Hurricanes and the escorting Blenheims arrived unscathed at Malta. Somerville flew his flag in *Ark Royal* for this operation, returning to *Nelson* for a further ferrying operation the following day, this time with *Ark Royal*, *Furious*, *Hermione* and six destroyers in company. The force was shadowed by Italian aircraft, which were not detected by radar, but the operation was otherwise uneventful. A total of forty-nine Hurricanes were flown to Malta on these two occasions.

MALTA CONVOY – SEPTEMBER 1941

The next major convoy for Malta, called Halberd, received careful preparation. To give additional cover two battleships from the Home Fleet, *Prince of Wales* and *Rodney*, would be deployed, along with cruisers and destroyers. The plan required the bombing of Italian ports and aerodromes to be maintained at a constant level before and during the operation so that there would be no indication that it was a cover for sea operations. Eight submarines would be deployed in the Sicilian area. Beaufighters would be reserved for operating on the final day of the passage, *Ark Royal* providing fighter protection the previous day. The Mediterranean Fleet would be kept at short notice during the operation in order to proceed to sea and be sighted steaming westward as soon as it was apparent that British forces in the western basin had been seen. It was hoped this would dissuade any westward movement of German air forces from Libya. Somerville also informed the Admiralty, perhaps with Spartivento in mind, that he intended to remain in close support of the convoy and not be drawn away from it by a speedier enemy, unless it should close the convoy or one of its capital ships be crippled by a substantial reduction in speed.

Furious and seven destroyers sailed from Gibraltar on 18 September, *Furious* bound for the USA to refit and the destroyers to meet and escort the approaching Halberd convoy (WS 11X). The whole operation was put at risk when, on the morning of 20 September, Italian two-man torpedoes made an attack on Gibraltar. *Nelson* and *Ark Royal* were targeted, but the boom defences and the regular dropping of scare charges proved effective. Only one penetrated into the harbour, exploding its charge under the tanker *Denbydale*, moored alongside the detached mole, where it remained as a hulk for the rest of the war. Two merchant ships anchored outside the harbour were also attacked, one being sunk and the other damaged.

Somerville played a deception trick on sailing. He remained in *Nelson* but his flag was hoisted in *Rodney* (the twin of *Nelson* with a similar profile); this could be seen through binoculars from Algeciras. *Nelson* left harbour on the evening of 24 September with the band playing 'home going' tunes and a farewell message purporting to come from him in *Rodney*, and the ship sailed westward escorted by three destroyers. It was subsequently established that the ruse had succeeded, for a time at least. *Nelson* returned with the convoy, passing through the Straits at night. The following day Cunningham sailed from Alexandria with three battleships, three cruisers and eight destroyers to give the impression that a convoy was being passed right through the Mediterranean and to draw enemy air effort away from Force H.

Escorting the convoy of nine merchant ships were three battleships (*Nelson*, *Prince of Wales* and *Rodney*), one aircraft carrier (*Ark Royal*), five cruisers (*Sheffield*, *Kenya*, *Edinburgh*, *Euryalus*, *Hermione*), and twenty destroyers which included the Dutch *Isaac Sweers* and the Polish *Piorun*. This was a major fleet operation in which four Admirals took part. Somerville asked only for Syfret, who had commanded the escort for the passage of the Substance convoy through the Narrows, but who in fact was the junior of the other two Admirals – Vice Admiral A. T. B. Curteis, second in command Home Fleet in *Prince of Wales*, and Rear Admiral H. M. Burrough, commanding 10th Cruiser Squadron in *Kenya*. The Italian fleet was for once matched by the reinforced Force H.

Next morning when in the Mediterranean the force split into two groups (as listed in Appendix 3) and further deception measures were taken. Group 1 proceeded eastwards so that if spotted it would appear to be Force H on a normal Club Run. Group 2, comprising the convoy and the two battleships, steered north-east towards the Balearics, keeping outside normal Italian air-reconnaissance cover. Both groups joined up on the morning of 27 September and assumed the formation shown opposite.

The first attack came that afternoon on the port side from six torpedo bombers. Two were shot down by barrage fire from *Rodney* and *Prince of Wales*, one by destroyers on the screen and one by fighters. Torpedoes were dropped about 5000 yards from the convoy, which altered course. Torpedo tracks showed up plainly and ships took heavy avoiding action. One passed within

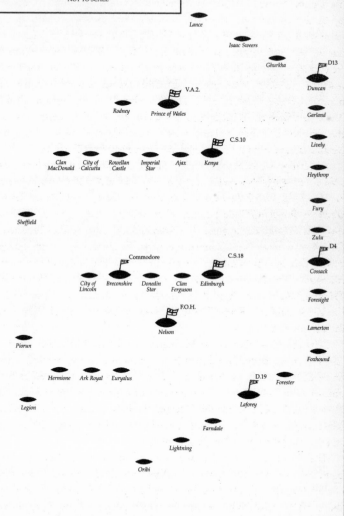

OPERATION HALBERD
FORMATION OF MALTA CONVOY
27 SEPTEMBER 1941

(Sketch from Journal of Midshipman
R.P. Dannreuther, HMS *Laforey*)

NOT TO SCALE

Lance

Isaac Sweers

Ghurkha

D13
Duncan

V.A.2.

Rodney   Prince of Wales

Garland

C.S.10

Lively

Clan   City of   Rowellan   Imperial   Ajax   Kenya
MacDonald Calcutta   Castle   Star

Heythrop

Fury

Sheffield

Zulu

D4
Commodore   C.S.18
Cossack

City of   Breconshire   Donedin   Clan   Edinburgh
Lincoln   Star   Ferguson

Foresight

F.O.H.

Lamerton

Nelson

Foxhound

Piorun

Hermione   Ark Royal   Euryalus

D.19
Forester

Legion

Laforey

Farndale

Lightning

Oribi

30 yards of *Lance* and another 100 yards to starboard of *Rodney* while she was swinging 60 degrees to port. Two Fulmars were shot down by their own ships' gunfire, and the crew of one was picked up.

The second attack, half an hour later at 1330, came from the starboard side of the convoy in the form of six or seven torpedo bombers. *Laforey* shot down one as it passed over the screen and three aircraft made a determined attack on *Nelson*. Somerville described what happened:[2]

> *Nelson* turned to starboard to comb the tracks and one passed parallel on the starboard side. The aircraft was hit by a pom pom as she whistled by, breaking into three pieces! The other dropped bang ahead about 400 yards off. I couldn't judge the angle but at the time thought it was 500–1 against a hit. However, when the bubbles appeared they were only about 120 yards dead ahead and coming straight for our stem, the torpedo apparently recovering from a deep dive. No possible avoiding action and I watched the bubbles disappear under the bows and then a tremendous 'crump', a column of water about 20 feet above the starboard rails before 'A' turret and the ship whipped like a fishing rod. I saw tracers going into this aircraft as it flashed by but didn't see it come down though I am told it eventually fell some way astern on the port quarter.

Nelson was seriously damaged, but she was not stopped. One aircraft was shot down by fighters and one Fulmar by *Rodney*'s pom-pom, the crew being rescued.

The third attack came a few minutes later from ten or eleven SM 79s but was not pressed home with the same determination as the earlier attacks. The aircraft split into two groups, one group retiring to the south-west when under fire from ships on the screen. The other group tried to work around the starboard bow but were turned away by the gunfire of the screening destroyers, dropping their torpedoes well outside the screen and at too great a range to endanger the convoy – though one torpedo narrowly missed *Lightning*. Three aircraft of the first group which had turned away came back astern of the convoy to attack *Ark Royal*. As the author recorded:[3]

> Two of them dropped their torpedoes well outside range and got clear, but the third with more guts than the rest came on in until I thought it was certain it would get the *Ark*. However the *Ark* blazed away at it and one shell must have gone straight through the fuselage, as it just

broke in half and fell into the sea. While all this was happening a Fiat fighter was drawing the fire of most of the ships on the starboard side of the screen by its queer antics. The Fiat was flying up and down outside the wing destroyers, soaring up to quite a height, almost stalling, and then diving down to sea level, and it did this repeatedly. If intended as a diversion it was not successful but as a lot of ships opened fire on it, it did waste valuable ammunition. The sky all around it was spotted with bursts, but it still went on climbing and diving. Ships eventually stopped firing and watched it continuing its performance until in one dive it failed to straighten out and crashed into the sea – an amusing finale, having got away unscathed and finally crashing without being hit.

Overall of the thirty torpedo bombers attempting to attack in 'a most hectic afternoon', only eighteen came within torpedo range. Seven aircraft were destroyed by gunfire and five by fighters.

While the third attack was still in progress an RAF reconnaissance plane from Malta reported an Italian force of two battleships, four cruisers and sixteen destroyers 75 miles to the north-east and steaming south at 20 knots. From this Somerville inferred that either the enemy did not realise there was more than one battleship with the convoy and intended to intercept it near the western entrance to the Skerki Channel, or that the enemy would try to draw away the escorting force to the north-eastwards, thus leaving the convoy open to attack by light forces in the Skerki Channel at dusk. He therefore hauled out in *Nelson* to intercept, taking *Prince of Wales, Rodney, Edinburgh, Sheffield* and six destroyers. Two Swordfish were flown off from *Ark Royal* to shadow the enemy. *Nelson* had to drop out as she could not make more than 15 knots, and Somerville ordered Curteis to proceed at best speed and drive off the enemy.

At this point the Italian Admiral had doubts about the aircraft reports he had received. Fearing that there might be more than one battleship in the British force and that he was steaming into a trap, he reversed course. The last report from the Swordfish shadowers was that the enemy was steering north-east. A further signal stating that the enemy had altered course to the north was not received by Malta or by the force. The battleships chased to the north-east and *Ark Royal* flew off a striking force in that direction of twelve Swordfish escorted by four Fulmars. They reported that they were unable to find the enemy ships and, with signs that they were retiring at high speed to the north-east, and that it was unlikely that contact would be made in

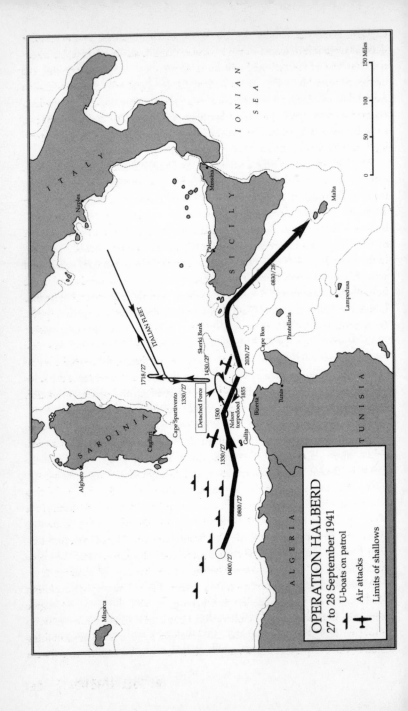

OPERATION HALBERD
27 to 28 September 1941

— — — U-boats on patrol

✈ Air attacks

········ Limits of shallows

0   50   100   150 Miles

SARDINIA

Cagliari

Alghero

Minorca

ALGERIA

TUNISIA

Tunis

Bizerta

Cape Bon

Pantellaria

Lampedusa

Malta

SICILY

Palermo

Messina

ITALY

Naples

IONIAN SEA

ITALIAN FLEET

Cape Spartivento

Skerki Bank

Galita

Detached Force

Nelson torpedoed

0400/27

0800/27

1330/27

1500

1855

2030/27

1430/27

1330/27

1718/27

0830/28

daylight, Somerville recalled the striking force. Even if contact was made after dark, a favourable outcome would have been hard to achieve. It was also essential that the cruisers should return to the convoy before dark, and the destroyers were required to screen *Nelson* and *Ark Royal*. Meanwhile the Italian Admiral received reports of the Italian air attack earlier in the afternoon which claimed a cruiser sunk, possibly a battleship sunk and two cruisers damaged, so he turned south again. There ensued the odd situation of both forces steering south 50 miles apart, unknown to each other. No action was joined.

At 1900 on reaching the entrance to the Skerki Channel the convoy with escorting cruisers and destroyers continued to the eastward under the command of Burrough in *Kenya*. The remaining ships retired to the west. Between 2000 and 2040 there were four torpedo-bomber attacks on the convoy, each by two or three aircraft. In the first attack an emergency turn to port together by the convoy was incorrectly transmitted and the columns turned outwards. In the second attack the aircraft formations crossed from starboard to port and attacked from the port beam. Three torpedo bombers in the third attack came from the port beam and one torpedo was seen to explode at the end of its run. In the fourth attack *Sheffield* had to turn under full rudder to avoid a torpedo, *Oribi* turned stern on and increased to full speed to avoid another, and at 2032 *Imperial Star* was hit by a torpedo port side aft. The aircraft was shot down by *Oribi*. All these attacks came from the port beam, although the moon was on the starboard quarter. The intensive gunfire and tracer from the ships lit up the area. The gun flashes probably showed up the convoy to aircraft manoeuvring to attack, and pointed to the need for flashless charges.

The convoy's route to Malta took it close to the Sicilian coast. *Hermione* was detached to carry out a bombardment of Pantellaria and laid on a spectacular diversion, seen by the convoy from 50 miles away. There were no attacks by E-boat as had been expected, and the unhindered night passage following the air attacks came as an anti-climax after the fierce fighting experienced by the Substance convoy two months earlier. Several formations of enemy aircraft were detected between dawn and the arrival of the convoy at Malta, but no attacks developed. The Beaufighter and Hurricane protection from Malta was excellent. The cruisers proceeded ahead to a warm welcome by the people of Malta, the convoy berthing later that day, 28 September.

All ships arrived safely, except for the *Imperial Star*. The torpedo explosion had blown away both propellers and her rudder, and the hold and engine room were flooded. *Heythrop* embarked her passengers and the ship was taken in tow by *Oribi*. But, although she could manage a speed of 8 knots, nothing could be done to prevent her steering in circles as a result of her damaged stern acting as a rudder. As it was impractical to tow the ship without tugs, which were not available at Malta, *Oribi* took off the crew, placed charges and with some gunfire assistance left her heavily on fire and listing badly. She sank later.

The damaged *Nelson*, meanwhile, had been sailing westward at 14 knots, slowing to 12 knots to reduce the strain on bulkheads and decks. *Prince of Wales*, *Rodney*, *Ark Royal* and destroyers awaited the return of the convoy's escort to Malta. The latter had sailed after refuelling and steamed close to the Tunisian coast, rounding Cape Bon. On joining up, the combined force sailed westward, keeping 40 miles from the African coast. *Lively* sighted a periscope and the submarine fired two torpedoes. Although *Lively* and *Legion* counter-attacked, the contact could not be regained and the hunt was abandoned. Later *Gurkha* detected and attacked a submarine in conjunction with *Legion*, and large amounts of wreckage soon surfaced that confirmed it to be an Italian U-boat. All ships returned to Gibraltar by 1 October.

Nelson docked immediately on arriving in harbour. She was 8 feet down by the bows and it was estimated that 3500 tons of water had entered the ship. In order to reduce her draft forward before docking, while on passage thirty-two shackles of cable, each of 15 fathoms and weighing over 3 tons, were got up from the cable lockers and manhandled aft to the waist of the ship. The torpedo had hit in the cold room and meat stores area. Somerville reported 'the great stink of 16 tons of rotting beef'. In another account it was noted: 'There is an amusing rumour going around that the German propagandists have been putting it about that 500 dead bodies are being got up out of HMS *Nelson* and that people in Gibraltar are complaining of the smell.'[4] The crew of the torpedo compartment in the bows of the ship had been withdrawn before the attack to help ammunition supply parties elsewhere and there were no casualties.

Concurrent with and part of the Halberd operation was the return to Gibraltar of three empty merchant ships from Malta which had formed part of the previous Substance convoy. *Melbourne Star* sailed on 26 September and made an uneventful passage, arriving in Gibraltar three days later. *Port Chalmers* and *City of Pretoria* sailed together on 27 September. Off Pantelleria during the night *Port Chalmers* engaged an E-boat, firing her stern 4-inch gun, and the enemy withdrew after six rounds fired. In the morning the ships hoisted French colours and continued separately. *City of Pretoria* was approached by three tor-pedo bombers. On going into action she hoisted British colours as was customary and engaged the aircraft, avoiding the three torpedoes that were dropped. While she was being machine-gunned by one of the aircraft, a periscope was sighted and a depth charge released. Later an unidentified vessel, possibly a submarine, followed the ship during the night and was engaged by gunfire. The ship then moved into territorial waters and the pursuer was shaken off. Both ships arrived at Gibraltar on 30 September. Their Masters were praised by Somerville for their resolute handling of their ships.

The convoy was a success, delivering 85,000 tons of cargo for the loss of one merchant ship and damage to one battleship, for which mishaps Somerville 'reprimanded and admonished his "guardian angel"'. He attributed the immunity from attack after passing the Skerki Channel to the route of the convoy close to the Sicilian coast, a new and untried track, the result of a bold suggestion by Admiral Ford, Flag Officer Malta. Somerville stressed the very considerable increased hazards if the passage was made in moonlight. At no time had enemy surface forces constituted a serious threat and the bombing and machine-gunning of enemy aerodromes in Sicily and Sardinia had reduced the scale of air attack. *Ark Royal*'s ability to maintain fighter patrols in the light variable wind conditions was an important factor in meeting the continuing air threat. RAF co-operation throughout had been excellent. Gunfire from destroyers on the screen had been effective and had encouraged air attacks to be made from abaft the beam. Barrage fire from 6-inch and 4-inch guns was especially devastating and accounted for at least four aircraft. At least one aircraft fell to pom-poms, but there was a general tendency for close-range weapons to fire astern and low. The effectiveness of the 6000-yard screen against torpedo bombers was demonstrated on the several occasions when aircraft tried to come in low over the destroyers and were turned back, only four aircraft facing their fire and pressing on. None was able to reach a good position to torpedo a ship of the convoy during the day attacks. *Nelson*'s lack of AA guns that would bear right ahead precluded any defence against attack from that direction.

So the two major Malta convoys, Substance and Halberd, had been very effective, with the loss of only one merchant ship – far fewer than had been anticipated. The withdrawal of the Luftwaffe from its bases in Sicily undoubtedly helped in achieving this low loss rate, but bearing in mind the surface, air, mining and E-boat threats in the Italian-dominated area through which the convoys had to pass, it was nonetheless a remarkable performance. The success of these operations in the western basin was helped by deception measures practised by Somerville, whether the devious departure routines on leaving Gibraltar or the misleading routes at sea of the whole or parts of the force.

With *Nelson* out of action in dock Somerville now hoisted his flag temporarily in *Rodney*. Together with *Ark Royal*, *Hermione* and seven destroyers,

Rodney carried out a Club Run on 16 October, when eleven Albacores and two Swordfish were flown through successfully to Malta. *Ark Royal*'s fighters shot down two shadowers. This operation also gave cover to Force K, consisting of cruisers *Aurora* and *Penelope* and destroyers *Lance* and *Lively* on passage to join the Mediterranean Fleet. These ships were to be in action very soon. In a fierce night action an Italian convoy of seven merchant ships and an escorting destroyer were sunk, with no casualties to the British ships. Also in October two merchant ships from the Halberd convoy, *City of Lincoln* and *Dunedin Star*, returned to Gibraltar, having successfully avoided torpedoes from torpedo bombers and driven off the enemy by gunfire. But *Empire Guillemot* was sunk on passage and her survivors were landed at Algiers. *Clan Ferguson* also sailed from Malta independently, but was sighted by enemy air reconnaissance and recalled to Malta. In the Atlantic the destroyer *Cossack* was torpedoed while escorting convoy HG 75 and sank later while under tow to Gibraltar. *Cossack* was a ship with a high reputation. Under Vian's command she had become well known for boarding the German tanker *Altmark* in a Norwegian fjord to rescue British seamen being taken to Germany, and for her part in the *Bismarck* action. The battleship *Malaya* arrived at Gibraltar to relieve *Rodney* and become Force H's new flagship. In view of her low speed, lack of endurance and paucity of AA armament, Somerville hoped her allocation to the force would be of short duration.

In his reports of the various actions in which Force H took part, Somerville frequently highlighted the personal achievements of officers and men who might be considered for awards for gallantry or outstanding service. In October he was himself honoured. After the Halberd convoy and taking into account the other Malta convoys, the bombardment of Genoa, the successful ferrying of Hurricanes and the *Bismarck* action, he was now high in Churchill's esteem and was appointed a Knight Commander of the Order of the British Empire. He was invested with his new title by King George VI when he returned to Britain at the end of October for consultation with the Admiralty. He was already a Knight Commander of the Order of the Bath and his new knighthood prompted his friend Cunningham at the other end of the Mediterranean to signal, 'What, twice a knight at your age?'

Such signals, which became widely known, cheered everybody up. Somerville had a gift for humour, and not only in his signals. Most of his jokes were passed on by word of mouth and did not find their way into print, but Donald Macintyre's biography of him, *Fighting Admiral*, published in 1961, gives a good idea of what it was like to serve under him. On one occasion, the shortage and rationing of water in Gibraltar prompted some WRNS officers to wangle their way aboard ship to have a hot bath. Their Officer in Charge put up a stern notice saying that Wrens were not to have baths on board HM Ships. Somerville, visiting the Wrennery shortly afterwards, saw the notice and wrote underneath, 'Except when visiting FO(H)'. Gibraltar was a small community and village gossip like this was much enjoyed. Another time, when the ships were approaching harbour the signal was sent, 'Please arrange Admiral's woman to be ready.' Somewhat mystified, Gibraltar asked for clarification. Somerville replied, 'Insert washer between Admiral and woman.' At sea when halyards in the flagship jammed the siren causing it to give a prolonged blast, which indicated an emergency turn, an apologetic flag signal was hoisted at the yardarm – 'PARDON'. Somerville also enjoyed the traditional repartee between the Army and the Navy. When *Renown* returned to Gibraltar after the *Bismarck* action, a soldier shouted across to the ship, 'So it takes all the bloody Navy to sink the *Bismarck*'; back went the reply, 'Only half, the other half's evacuating you bastards from Crete.'

In this context of light banter between the services, it was the Navy at Gibraltar during the war which coined the term 'Pongo' to describe a soldier, of whatever persuasion and of whatever rank. The word is derived from those other defenders of the Rock, the legendary apes whose continued presence is held to ensure that the Rock stays British. Pongo was an early name for a large African anthropoid ape, with which the Barbary apes of Gibraltar may be associated. The word was widely used, not least in some of Somerville's letters, and could be interpreted as a term of affection or abuse as the occasion required. No animosity was intended or implied, rather as a Swordfish was referred to as a Stringbag.

THE LOSS OF *ARK ROYAL*

In preparation for the next Club Run, *Argus* and the auxiliary transport *Athene* brought out Hurricanes to Gibraltar. In the escort were *Laforey* (leader of the 19th Destroyer Flotilla) and *Lightning*, concluding the relief of the Fs by the Ls. The latter were newly completed ships with a much more effective AA armament. *Malaya*, *Ark Royal*, *Argus*, *Hermione* and seven destroyers sailed on 10 November. Bad weather at Gibraltar prevented the escorting Blenheims from taking off and delayed the operation for twenty-seven hours. The ships had to remain at sea in an exposed position during this period. The Hurricanes, twenty-six from *Ark Royal* and eleven from *Argus*, were flown off in two waves of nineteen and eighteen; three failed to arrive at Malta. Ominously for Force H, it was about this time that Fliegerkorps X of the Luftwaffe was ordered back to Sicily from Greece in order to operate against

Malta and British naval forces. The latter had been inflicting heavy losses on supply convoys to Libya. A strong force of U-boats was also ordered into the Mediterranean.

After a Club Run, Force H usually returned to Gibraltar along either the Spanish or Moroccan coasts, making the final approach from the north-east or the south-east. As this practice was probably known to the enemy, and U-boats had been reported in the area, on this occasion Somerville approached directly from the east. It was to prove a fateful decision.

Various A/S contacts were detected and attacked and *Ark Royal* kept well inside the screen during flying operations. Apart from *Hermione* being detached to act as a target for a throw-off shoot by *Malaya*, the screen was intact, and inner and outer A/S patrols were being flown. But in the afternoon, when only 30 miles from Gibraltar, *Ark Royal* was hit by a torpedo on the starboard side. The explosion was so severe that aircraft on the forepart of her flight deck jumped up clear of the deck and then bounced a couple of times.

The hydrophone effect of propeller noise had been heard in a destroyer on the screen but was not reported, as it was thought to be that from a nearby destroyer. *Malaya* and *Argus*, escorted by three destroyers, continued to Gibraltar, the remaining destroyers forming a protective screen around *Ark Royal*, now stopped with a 20-degree list having lost all steam and with black smoke pouring from her funnel. Her great flight deck at this angle made the hit seem more severe and *Legion* was called alongside to take off most of her crew. A larger number of the fire and repair parties left the ship than had been intended, due to the breakdown of the broadcast system and misunderstanding of the orders given,[5] and eighty of these key officers and ratings had to be recovered from *Legion* before she could proceed to Gibraltar; every bit of space in the destroyer was crammed full.

Hermione closed to transfer a portable pump with hoses, and *Laforey* then went alongside to supply power and to pump over 25 tons of boiler feed water so that steam could be raised in one unit which had been closed down; No. 2 boiler room was flooded. The sea fortunately was calm. The ship had been torpedoed in daylight and had not been battened down for the night. It was pitch dark by now and as power was gradually restored lights came on in the hanger and in scuttles in the hull and superstructure which had not been closed. The ship stood out like a lighthouse, further illuminated by flare-ups when the power leads supplying 1000 amps from *Laforey* chafed through; this happened three times. Eventually the ship raised steam and was able to produce her own power. Tugs arrived from Gibraltar and a slow tow of 3 to 4 knots was achieved. The flooding was under control and all looked promising. But shortly after midnight steam was lost. A leaking oil-fuel pipe from the damage caused by the torpedo started a fire in the boiler room and flooding of the funnel uptakes got out of control. A tug went alongside with another pump and was joined by *Laforey*. Somerville returned from Gibraltar in a destroyer to board *Laforey* at 0430 when on the point of casting off, having taken off *Ark Royal*'s Captain and the last of the steaming party. The ship was by now listing 35 degrees. Then, to the distress of all those watching, she turned over and sank at 0613. On capsizing, a hole measuring 120 to 150 feet long and 30 feet wide became visible between the starboard bilge keel and the centre-line of the ship. There were 1739 survivors; one rating was killed and one seriously injured.

All in Force H felt her loss deeply, and no one more so than Somerville. To his wife he wrote, 'It was the blackest of days when I saw my poor *Ark* sink at 6 a.m. this morning. Just a blur in the dark as she lay on her side for some time and then slowly, slowly she turned over like a tired and wounded ship going to sleep. … I am rather cut up about this because I was so proud and fond of my *Ark*. As I signalled to the Admiralty this gallant ship has paid a fine dividend during the war, and her loss is deeply regretted.'[6]

She was a great ship, a very efficient and happy one, with an impressive war record and wonderful fighting spirit. She carried a lot of prestige, both at home, where she was a household name especially after her fine performance in the *Bismarck* action and in Mediterranean operations, and abroad. Nazi and Italian propaganda had waged a vendetta against her, proclaiming her sunk many times. The traitor-broadcaster Lord Haw Haw's taunts of 'Where is the *Ark Royal* now?' had always met with a ready response on the mess decks. At this time Warship Weeks were being held in Britain. Leeds decided to make an effort to raise the £3.5 million necessary to replace the ship. Liverpool, set to raise £10 million in adopting the new battleship *Prince of Wales*, was encouraged by the First Lord of the Admiralty to raise the cost of a new carrier as well.[7] Such was the esteem in which the ship was held. Gibraltar felt her loss keenly. There had been considerable bonding, to use the modern term, between the *Ark* and the Rock, and it was poignant to see her berth empty in harbour. She was the third ship of that name in the Navy and it continues to be associated with the Fleet Air Arm, the fourth and fifth ships both being aircraft carriers.

There were some hard lessons to be learnt from her sinking. A ship of her size, after being towed for several hours in fine weather, should have been able to survive a single torpedo hit. There were contributing causes: the telephone exchange and main switchboard were put out of action simultaneously; no diesel generators were fitted, only turbo generators which cannot provide power when steam is lost; a manhole in a main hatch over the switchboard room had been left open, and individual funnel uptakes were not made water-tight, an omission in design which allowed the flooding to spread.[8] With the ship listing to starboard the funnel uptake was sealed by water, preventing steam being raised. Without steam it was almost impossible to deal with the flooding onboard.

In terms of Force H *Ark Royal* was of course the vital component and her loss was a crippling blow. *Indomitable*, whom it had been intended should be her relief, was now being used instead to ferry Hurricanes to the Far East. With no replacement carrier available, the force had little to do in the ensuing weeks and was confined to harbour, except for some periods of exercising at sea. The destroyers however continued to be needed for the anti-submarine patrols carried out in the approaches to the Straits, to which the highest priority was given. A dummy convoy of six merchant ships with six escorts sailed into the Mediterranean on the evening of 16 November, the convoy returning to Gibraltar independently during the night while the escorts carried out an anti-submarine sweep to the eastward. Also on 16 November, *Nelson* and three destroyers sailed for Britain, taking with them the majority of survivors from *Ark Royal* and *Cossack*. On 11 December four destroyers sailed for Malta to join the Mediterranean Fleet. They were fol-lowed ten days later by a cruiser and five destroyers. On Christmas Day Somerville visited all ships under his command and, unlike in 1940, the day was spent in harbour. All the ships had changed in the intervening year, however, and only the staff could remember the previous Christmas. But two air-raid alerts in the afternoon and evening, requiring all forces to stand to, served as reminders that no relaxation was permitted on that day. The end of the year was enlivened by the Admiralty reporting that photo-recon-naissance of Brest had failed and that the possibility could not be ignored that *Gneisenau* might attempt to make the passage of the Straits. Force H was brought to two hours' notice for steam.

THE AXIS ADVANCE AND U-BOAT ACTIVITY

The sinking of the *Ark* in November sharply reversed the more favourable out-look held in the autumn, and heralded the start of a calamitous period of the war at sea. A fortnight after the loss of the carrier, the battleship *Barham* was torpedoed and sunk in the eastern Mediterranean with a heavy loss of life. In December in Alexandria harbour two battleships, *Queen Elizabeth* and

Valiant, were attacked by two-man submarines, which inflicted so much damage that the ships were out of action for a year. Also in December in the eastern Mediterranean the cruiser *Galatea* was sunk by torpedo, followed a few days later by the loss in a minefield of three of the four Force K ships, which arrived on station in October, only *Penelope* remaining. And in the Far East, again in December, the capital ships *Prince of Wales* and *Repulse* were sunk by Japanese air attack off Singapore. In those few weeks more than a third of Britain's capital-ship strength was lost, and the Mediterranean Fleet was reduced to three light cruisers and a few destroyers. But this was not all. In December the Japanese dramatically attacked Pearl Harbor and sank or put out of action seven battleships of the US Navy. The combined strength of the two Navies was reduced by twelve capital ships. Against these disasters was set the comforting knowledge that America was now in the war with Britain, and there could be no doubt of its outcome.

The next six months marked the height of the Axis successes. Rommel and the Afrika Korps were 60 miles from Cairo; the German Army reached Rostok on the Don; Singapore fell; in south-east Asia British forces were driven out of Burma and the overland route to China was severed; and in the Pacific the Japanese occupied the Solomons and Aleutians. It was a dire period of the war for the Allies, made worse by the severe shipping losses inflicted by U-boats in the Atlantic and the heavy demands made by the Arctic convoys carrying supplies to Russia.

In the latter part of 1941 German U-boats had begun to concentrate in the Atlantic approaches to Gibraltar. At the end of September the first group passed through the Straits into the Mediterranean. It was suggested that *Ark Royal* and her aircraft should be used to protect the convoys in areas where there had been persistent attacks. Somerville pointed out that the endurance of the destroyers would restrict such operations to one day unless they could be refuelled, that the prospects of refuelling in those areas were not good, and that *Ark Royal* was only suitable for refuelling destroyers in good weather. Also *Hermione*, who would be required as escort for *Ark Royal*, had poor endurance and would have to be refuelled at sea. He concluded that the risks involved to *Ark Royal* did not justify the results likely to be achieved. The second group of U-boats, to which the ship fell prey, passed through the Straits in November and a third group at the end of the month.

Attacks on the convoy routes to and from Gibraltar became more frequent. Responsibility for this shipping lay with the Admiral Commanding the North Atlantic Station at Gibraltar. In November and December when there was a lull in U-boat activity in the Atlantic, only twenty-seven U-boats covered the whole ocean and twelve of these were concentrated in the approaches to Gibraltar. Wolf-pack attacks were made on the convoys, which at one time had to be suspended. Anti-submarine patrols in the Straits and the approaches were intensified, in which Force H destroyers took part, as did some of *Ark Royal*'s radar-fitted aircraft which had been airborne when the ship was hit and had landed at Gibraltar. Water conditions in the Straits made it difficult to detect submarines, who naturally preferred to make the passage submerged. But before they could do so they had to surface to recharge their batteries; this was before schnorkels were widely fitted. Accordingly an outer patrol line was established in the Atlantic waters between Cape Spartel and Cape Trafalgar, as it was accepted that a Straits patrol would be unable to prevent the submarines passing through.

In these sweeps and in support of convoys to and from Gibraltar, *Nestor* sank a U-boat on 15 December. On 17 December an A/S patrol aircraft from the escort carrier *Audacity* sighted a U-boat but was shot down while attacking; escorts from the convoy then sank the U-boat and took fifty-five prisoners. Later that day another U-boat was sunk by *Stork*. On 18 December *Blankney* and *Stanley* attacked a U-boat which dived but subsequently surfaced and was rammed by *Blankney*. On 19 December *Stanley* was torpedoed and sunk while searching for a submarine sighted earlier in the evening; in attempting to escape, the submarine surfaced and was rammed by *Stork*, completing a hat trick for the latter. On 21 December a Swordfish sank a U-boat off Cape Spartel. But despite these sinkings there were now about thirty U-boats operating in the Mediterranean.

SYFRET RELIEVES SOMERVILLE

Towards the end of the year Somerville began to look for a successor to relieve him. Much had now changed, particularly in the ships which had formed the hard core of the force. As we have noted, *Nelson* had replaced *Renown* as flagship when the latter returned to Britain for a refit; *Malaya* later became flagship after *Nelson*'s torpedoing in the Halberd convoy; *Sheffield* was relieved by *Hermione*; and the L class destroyers had taken over from the F class. Only *Ark Royal* had remained of the original squadron and with her loss the whole spirit and comradeship which had been the special hallmark of the force had, for the time being, gone. Somerville was also coming to the conclusion at this stage that Force H should be made part of the North Atlantic command. The Senior Officer, preferably based ashore, should be responsible for deciding how the available forces, especially the destroyers, should be employed.

Somerville at last ended his outstandingly successful time in command of

Force H on 3 January 1942, leaving Gibraltar in *Hermione* to return to Britain. The regime which he had set up lasted a further three months. *Hermione* was back in Gibraltar on 14 January, having brought out the new Flag Officer Force H, Rear Admiral E. N. Syfret. Syfret had taken the ships through to Malta in both the Substance and Halberd convoys and Somerville was very pleased to have him as his relief. Somerville's flag was not struck on his departure but was kept flying so as not to alert the binocular-watchers in Algeciras that change might be afoot. Without a carrier and no Club Run planned, it was an unaccustomedly idle time for the flagship. *Malaya* remained in harbour until 8 February. AA firing and 15-inch sub-calibre firing practices were carried out across the mole on targets in the Bay; route marches were held, led by the band, through the tunnel to Sandy Bay and round the Rock; and a regatta and pantomime were organised. But, as usual, the small ships were not allowed such respite and continued to undertake the anti-submarine patrols against U-boats passing through the Straits. One German submarine on the surface was rammed and sunk.

At the end of January 1942 there were once again indications that the two German battlecruisers in Brest, *Gneisenau* and *Scharnhorst*, were preparing for sea. The Admiralty assessed they might make another sortie into the Atlantic or return to Germany up the English Channel. Another WS convoy, an important troop convoy of twenty-six large ships carrying 40,000–50,000 soldiers, was due to sail for the Middle East, and Force H, consisting of *Malaya*, *Hermione* and seven destroyers, sailed on 8 February to return home to escort it. On the day the force arrived back in the Clyde the battlecruisers did leave Brest, but sailed up the Channel and, although not unscathed, successfully returned to Germany, where they would be better placed for the Allied attack on Norway that Hitler feared. This caused immense indignation in Britain, newspaper sarcasm contrasting the German success with the failure of the Duke of Medina Sidonia and his Armada three and a half centuries before. But while it was seen as a humiliating defeat, there is no doubt that the removal of the ships from Brest was to Britain's advantage as it greatly reduced the pressure on those protecting the convoy routes. The German naval staff correctly assessed it as a tactical victory for them but a strategic defeat. The troop convoy WS 16 sailed on 17 February, with the Force H ships, now including *Eagle*, leaving it four days later to return to Gibraltar.

Argus meanwhile had been given an operational role and embarked eight Swordfish and two Hurricanes. On 27 February *Malaya*, *Eagle*, *Argus*, *Hermione* and eight destroyers sailed for a Club Run, but it had to be aborted due to defects in aircraft fuel tanks. The operation was repeated on 6 March when *Eagle* flew off fifteen Spitfires. This was the first occasion when Spitfires were flown through. All planes and their Blenheim escorts arrived safely.

The war being fought on the other side of the world now intruded. After the Japanese successes at Pearl Harbor and Singapore, the Indian Ocean had become a vulnerable area. It was vital to maintain the Middle East convoy route from South Africa up to the Red Sea. The island of Madagascar, under Vichy French control, was strategically sited to command the southern Indian Ocean. It would be disastrous if Diego Suarez, the excellent natural harbour at the north end of the island, fell into enemy hands. At short notice a force was assembled in Britain for an assault 9000 miles away by three infantry brigade groups and a Commando. It had always been envisaged that Force H might be required in the Indian Ocean in certain circumstances, and these had now arisen. Syfret was appointed Commander-in-Chief of the Combined Force and sailed in *Malaya* with *Hermione* and five destroyers to join the assault force forming part of convoy WS 17A.

On leaving Gibraltar on 1 April 1942 the Force H title lapsed and Syfret became Senior Officer of Force F for Operation Ironclad, the attack on Diego Suarez. He retained that title for his subsequent planning and command of the largest and most fiercely fought through Malta convoy in August 1942, Operation Pedestal. Force H was subsequently reconstituted under his command for the invasion of North Africa later that year. It did not then have the distinction of being a detached squadron under the direct control of the Admiralty, but came under the orders of the naval Commander-in-Chief in the normal way. Brief details of those events are given in the Epilogue.

EXERCISING SEA POWER

STRATEGICALLY, **FORCE H** met the demands made on it. While it acted as the security guard of the western entrance to the Mediterranean no enemy surface ships passed through the Straits. Its only significant lapse was the transit of French warships before the Dakar expedition, a muddle in which the Admiralty was also involved. The Admiralty's fears at various times that the battlecruisers *Scharnhorst* and *Gneisenau* and the battleships *Richelieu* and *Jean Bart* might attempt the passage were not realised, no doubt partly because of the deterrent presence of Force H at Gibraltar. Responsibility for preventing the passage of U-boats lay with the Admiral Commanding the North Atlantic Station, but Force H destroyers were deployed to assist in patrols whenever available.

The essential lines of communication through the Mediterranean were kept open by the reinforcement of warships to the Mediterranean Fleet, but the passage of merchant ships was all but halted. An exception was made when the delivery of their cargoes was deemed to be so essential as to justify the risks. There were three such small convoys of fast MT ships carrying military supplies, strongly escorted, and later two larger convoys with stores for the relief of Malta, for which the force was heavily reinforced. They were successful in that, overall, in these five convoys totalling twenty-six merchant ships, only two were lost and two damaged. Cunningham saw Force H as a potent factor in the operations of the eastern Mediterranean Fleet. Besides its value as an Atlantic force, it was a standing threat to any seaborne expedition to North Africa. He considered the maintenance of a heavy ship force at Gibraltar of great importance.[1]

Opportunities for offensive operations in the western Mediterranean were limited. The bombardment of Genoa was the most audacious and succeeded despite the risks involved. Otherwise Somerville had to be content with passing strikes at airfields in Sardinia by *Ark Royal*'s aircraft. However, it must be remembered that the Italians had superiority in their naval and air forces and every foray into the Mediterranean, be it to escort a convoy or to fly off Hurricanes, was itself an offensive action against the enemy. The Club Runs were also an expression of sea power being exerted in an unusual manner. The ability to project air power in this way into a hostile area cut off from normal routes of supply represented a new concept in modern warfare. Some Hurricanes were lost in flight, but maintenance of fighter strength in Malta was a salient factor in the island's survival.

The image of the Battle of the Atlantic is of the unrelenting struggle to protect convoys from U-boat attack. In this context Force H was not suitably equipped and could play no part. But the shipping also had to be protected from attack by German warships. Besides the normal mercantile convoys there were the special fast troop WS convoys of big ships bound for the Middle East, sailing around the Cape. With the large number of personnel being carried they were tempting targets and had to be escorted by a battleship or cruiser(s). The safety of the north–south Atlantic shipping routes relied on Gibraltar, and Force H was strategically well sited to give additional support when needed on their outward passage from Britain to Freetown. In the first half of 1941 the force spent much of its time on this duty either chasing reported enemy raiders and escorting convoys, or patrolling off Brest in conjunction with the Home Fleet in case the German heavy ships decided on another Atlantic sortie. No action was joined, not least because of the Germans' reluctance to get involved in an encounter which might cause them damage far from home. The enemy successes were mainly confined to attacks on unescorted convoys or ships individually routed. The fact that the troop convoys were not seriously interfered with demonstrated the true significance of maritime power.[2]

The main event for Force H in the Atlantic was the *Bismarck* action. Initially ordered to cover a troop convoy as part of the initial deployments made by the Admiralty, the force found itself in due course as the final barrier in preventing the enemy reaching Brest. And *Ark Royal* carried out its task magnificently in well-nigh impossible conditions. That the Swordfish, an obsolescent biplane, should have been the weapon to cripple the most powerful battleship afloat was a feat of David and Goliath proportions.

The Navy was unlike the other services in that the Admiralty was an operational control centre and could issue orders direct to Senior Officers. Although it was the generally agreed practice that Commanders-in-Chief should be left free to conduct their operations without interference from Whitehall, the status of Force H as a detached squadron did not allow such protection. The filter from political intrusion normally provided by orders coming from a Commander-in-Chief was not available to Somerville, who felt strongly that the orders he was receiving from the Admiralty lacked the singleness of purpose he could properly expect. Much of this related to the actions to be taken against the French, generally because of the political interest in dealing with French warships and merchant ships and the uncertainty of how to implement the various policies decided upon. Some of the blame must be attributed to Churchill, well known for his tendency to involve himself in operational matters.

Force H may also be seen as a forerunner of the modern concept of a task force, in which all ships are interdependent. Naval command at sea was traditionally exercised through admirals in command of different types of squadron – battleship, battlecruiser, aircraft carrier, cruiser squadrons – all under the control of the commander-in-chief. With ships in each class subordinate to the one authority, this was a convenient arrangement. Somerville in command of Force H, with an increased staff, was the administrative authority for all the ships in his force, and the autonomy given him as a detached squadron under the Admiralty's direct control widened his authority compared to that of admirals of other squadrons. With his ability to command and control operations of fleet strength in his region, he was effectively acting as a commander of a fleet – a status ascribed to Force H by Stephen Roskill in his *The War at Sea*.[3]

The outstanding success of the two large Malta convoys gave clear demonstration of the proficiency Force H had achieved. The force may be said to have peaked with the first, the Substance convoy, when the hard-core elements that had formed the squadron in its early days were still present – *Renown* the flagship, *Ark Royal* and the 8th Destroyer Flotilla. Only *Sheffield*, relieved by *Hermione* just beforehand, was missing. After one year of working together, the ships had been successfully welded by Somerville into an effective fighting force – to such an extent that other ships joining from the Home Fleet readily fell into the operating procedures and doctrines he had established, not least in the new field of radar-assisted air defence of the fleet which he pioneered. This point is important because of the influence Force H thereby exerted on other ships in the Navy. Appendix 3 gives the names of the 124 ships which took part in operations with the force, representing some 50,000--55,000 men. For these ships' companies, the threat of sustained and deadly air attacks in the Mediterranean was of a different order to that experienced in the Atlantic where the air threat was less apparent, and provided the stimulus for ships to strive for and maintain full fighting efficiency. The deployment of Home Fleet ships to the Mediterranean for a Force H operation helped a significant number of ships in the Navy to achieve overall operational proficiency. In this context the force was held in respect in the Home Fleet. The reputation the squadron had gained was also noted by the Home Fleet which, with the Atlantic as their battleground, lacked the glamour that resulted from the frequent press reporting of activities in the western Mediterranean. In some ways this repeated the feeling experienced in the Grand Fleet twenty-five years earlier when the Battle Cruiser Force, based at Rosyth and nearer the enemy, had most of the excitement that the war provided and was more experienced than the main fleet based at Scapa Flow.[4] But the rivalries and jealousies that were generated among those ships in the First World War found no place in the relationship between the Home Fleet and Force H in the Second.

These remarks should not be interpreted as implying that Force H was a wonder squadron, always in the thick of fighting. For the final eight months of this account it operated mostly in the Mediterranean, but in the first half of 1941 it spent much time in the Atlantic. Nor, in terms of being in action against the enemy, can it be compared with the losses and punishing casualties suffered by the Mediterranean Fleet. Somerville's ships attracted publicity but, as he pointed out to Churchill, who had been favourably commenting on the number of times the force had been engaged on operations, he had an occasional run whereas Cunningham's ships were always in action and suffered incomparably greater strain.[5]

Britain was fortunate to have had two such able and resolute men as Cunningham and Somerville at either end of the Mediterranean during this difficult time. As always a force reflects its leadership. Somerville was described in *The Times* during the war, accurately and succinctly, as 'an inspiring leader, skilful commander and fighting Admiral'. He insisted on careful planning of operations, which were undertaken only after full examination of the risks. Captains knew that no ship would ever be left unsupported or misused. A continuing theme in the books written on ships in the squadron is the remarkable faith of the officers and men in their Admiral. The confidence which this instilled found expression in the equally remarkable rapport and esprit de corps of the force. When this was combined with its high state of efficiency and experience of action the result was a strong, effective and reliable fighting unit. The squadron was so tightly knit that Somerville was as synonymous with Force H just as much as Force H was synonymous with *Ark Royal*. It was a combination which earned and deserved its reputation in the Navy.

Force H demonstrated how sea power can be exercised. Here was a squadron of ships, a composite force experienced in all forms of naval warfare, based in a strategic position from which it was ready to sail at a few hours' notice either to the north-east to attack the enemy's mainland, in the bombardment of Genoa; or to the east to succour a besieged island, in the Malta convoys and the Club Runs; or to the south (as Force F) to carry out an opposed landing 7000 miles away at Diego Suarez; or to the south-west in response to French warship movements and to assist in the attack on Dakar; or to the west to protect Atlantic shipping and troop convoys and to hunt for enemy raiders; or to the north-west to fight a major fleet action against the *Bismarck*. And this is not to forget that the force was the instrument which accomplished what Churchill described, tragedy though it was, as a turning point in the war in the destruction of the French Fleet at Oran. The squadron was a prime example of the effectiveness and flexibility of sea power.

During Somerville's eighteen months in command, Gibraltar was Force H's base. The great mass of the Rock sighted from afar when approaching from the Mediterranean, or with more immediate and dramatic effect when arriving from the Atlantic, exerts a powerful presence. Its very British character has evolved over the years and nowhere has its influence been felt more than in its steadfastness as an anchorage and base for Britain's maritime affairs. For the last few hundred years it has provided substance for the many expeditions and adventures in these waters which have enriched the country's naval history and tradition. Here British sea power has made its impact since the days of Drake in the sixteenth century through Rooke, Rodney, Howe, Boscawen, St Vincent, Collingwood and Nelson, each with his ship or squadron or fleet. To that list must now be added Somerville and his Force H.

EPILOGUE

SOMERVILLE

TOWARDS THE END of his time in Force H, Somerville was not expecting another big appointment and, being on the Retired List, he expressed himself ready to serve anywhere and under anyone. This was very soon after Japan entered the war in December 1941 and Britain had lost two capital ships off Singapore under admirals who had no wartime experience at sea. Churchill wanted a fighting and experienced admiral out east and had no misgivings in selecting Somerville.

Somerville was promoted admiral, still retired, and appointed Commander-in-Chief of the Eastern Fleet; again causing some eyebrows to be raised at the prospect of a major fleet command being given in wartime to a retired officer. But by now his reputation was firmly established. It proved a most difficult and trying time and he was given only very slender resources. There were few opportunities to carry out offensive operations. One was a raid on Sabang in Sumatra in April 1944 when he achieved complete surprise, rather like his attack on Genoa three years earlier. Afterwards there was a typical Somerville signal to the fleet – 'We caught the Nips with their heads down and their kimonos up.'

After two years in that appointment, by which time he had hoisted his flag at sea longer than any other British admiral during the war, he was sent to head the British Admiralty Delegation in Washington. Staff work was not his mètier and the job did not appeal to him; he wrote, 'the thought fills me with gloom – I'd rather command a trawler'.

While he was there, in December 1944, he was at last reinstated on the Active List, and as a full admiral. It therefore became possible a few months later, on VE Day itself, 8 May 1945, and in recognition of his great service to his country, for him to be promoted Admiral of the Fleet, the highest rank in the Navy – to the lasting satisfaction and delight of all who knew him and had served with him.

APRIL–OCTOBER 1942

When Force H was first formed at the end of June 1940 a new Command was created for the force. Although the Force H title lapsed when the ships left Gibraltar on 1 April 1942, the Command remained in being and existed until October 1943. Syfret relieved Somerville in command of Force H but after 1 April 1942 his authority was vested in command of Force F, and he remained in command after Force H was reconstituted six months later.

During this period in the first half of 1942 the plight of Malta became increasingly precarious. A Luftwaffe wing had been transferred from the Russian front and Malta was being hit at the rate of over 6000 tons of bombs a month. Heavy attacks in April destroyed or damaged 126 aircraft, and twenty more were lost in air combat; the total losses suffered by the Malta-based RAF amounted to the virtual extinction of the island's air strength. Relief came from a Club Run when the US carrier *Wasp* sailed on 13 April to fly off forty-seven Spitfires, all but one reaching Malta. She was escorted by *Renown* under the command of Commodore C. S. Daniel and two cruisers from the Home Fleet, and by US and British destroyers. Some fighters were destroyed on the ground soon after they landed and there were delays in getting them airborne to meet the fierce air attacks then being made on the island. The trip was repeated on 8 May when *Wasp* again flew off forty-seven Spitfires together with seventeen from *Eagle*, and all but three of the sixty-four planes arrived. This time there were improved arrangements for their reception and heavy losses were inflicted on the Luftwaffe. It was a decisive moment in the battle for the island. The gesture by Britain's new ally in making one of its carriers available at a critical time in its fortunes in the Pacific was much appreciated. Later in May seventeen more Spitfires were flown off by *Eagle* and another fifty-five in two trips in June. Malta could not have survived without these repeated performances by this splendid old ship and the *Wasp*'s two sorties. For all these operations the carriers were escorted by ships of the Home Fleet.

There had been no major Malta relief convoy since the Halberd convoy in September 1941 and it began to look as if the island might be starved into defeat; there were a quarter of a million civilians and 50,000 servicemen in an area smaller than the Isle of Wight. The relief of Malta was therefore high on the agenda. Its fall would have had incalculable effects and there was no doubt in the minds of those fighting in the Mediterranean that the risks being run in keeping the island supplied were abundantly justified. The King's award of the George Cross to the island in April that year gave full recognition to the resilience of its people, in which were included the defending forces.

In June 1942 a larger-scale operation was planned for convoys to be run simultaneously to Malta from Gibraltar and Alexandria. The Gibraltar convoy, codeword Harpoon, consisted of six merchant ships and was escorted by *Malaya*, *Eagle* and *Argus*, all old ships of First World War construction and of limited capacity. There were about the same number of cruisers and destroyers as in previous convoys and the force, known as Force T, was commanded by Vice Admiral A. T. B. Curteis, Flag Officer Second-in-Command Home Fleet, in *Kenya*. Before it reached the Sicilian Narrows this convoy came under more sustained attack than its predecessors, and one merchant ship was sunk. Next day on the final approach to Malta three more ships were lost by mining and air attack. Only two of the six ships arrived, delivering 25,000 tons of cargo. The convoy from Alexandria had eleven merchant ships, with ships withdrawn from the Eastern Fleet to escort it. There were heavy losses from the outset. Two merchant ships were sunk and two damaged, and in the escort one cruiser, *Hermione*, and three destroyers were sunk and two corvettes damaged. Such a rate of loss could not be sustained, and, with ammunition running out, the convoy had to turn back. No ships reached Malta.

The familiarity which Home Fleet ships had by now acquired with operating in the western Mediterranean allowed these operations – the *Wasp* ferryings, the Club Runs and the Harpoon convoy – to be carried out without the experienced presence of Force H. This supports Somerville's view that the force had fulfilled its purpose as a detached squadron and that, while there was still a need for a force to be based at Gibraltar, the western Mediterranean requirements could now be met by normal deployments from the Home Fleet.

During this period Syfret with Force F had been engaged in the Madagascan operation. After leaving Gibraltar the ships refuelled at Freetown. At Cape Town he transferred his flag to *Illustrious* and later to *Ramillies* in Durban, where the force was further strengthened by *Indomitable* and other ships from the Eastern Fleet. *Malaya* returned to Gibraltar. It is outside the scope of this book to describe the assault on Diego Suarez, which was launched on 5 May. Suffice to say that it was a hard-fought but successful operation, and was in fact the first successful combined operation on any scale in the war. It was an all-British affair and there were no French troops: the memory of the fiasco at Dakar still rankled.

Towards the end of May, when the operation had achieved its purpose, the Admiralty announced that Force H was to be reconstituted when circumstances permitted with *Malaya*, *Eagle*, an AA cruiser and three destroyers; Syfret was to return to Gibraltar and resume duty as Senior Officer Force H but retain the title of Senior Officer Force F until resuming command of Force H.[1] In the event this proved to be wishful thinking. Syfret left Diego Suarez in *Ramillies* for Durban in early June, embarking later in *Canton* for passage to Freetown and thence to Gibraltar. But on passage he received an urgent summons from the Admiralty and he and his Staff Officer Operations flew home from Takoradi in West Africa. His flag was transferred to *Nelson* at Freetown and she later sailed for Scapa.

With only two ships reaching Malta from the convoys in June, the island was in a very grave predicament. There were just two months' supplies remaining, though Lord Gort, now the Governor in Malta, thought they might hold out for three months. There was therefore the need for a major effort to take supplies to the island and it was for this purpose that Syfret, now Vice Admiral, was recalled. He was required to plan the next convoy before commanding the operation. The convoy, codename Pedestal, from Gibraltar to Malta in August, was the most fiercely fought through of all the Malta convoys. Nine of the fourteen merchant ships were sunk in very heavy air attacks. Among the warships, the aircraft carrier *Eagle*, two cruisers and one destroyer were sunk; and another aircraft carrier, two cruisers and four destroyers were damaged. The convoy is remembered for the tanker *Ohio* being towed into Valletta with a destroyer lashed to each side. Much of the credit for the convoy getting through at all must be given to the immense care taken beforehand by Syfret in planning the operation. The story of his command of the operation, flying his flag in *Nelson*, is told in other books.

FORCE H RECONSTITUTED

It was not until October that the title of Force H was reconstituted. In the Pink List, the twice-weekly Most Secret bulletin issued by the Admiralty giving the dispositions of all major warships, there is no mention of Force H between April and November. There was no Force H presence at Gibraltar during this period, as asserted in some historical accounts. On 17 October the flag of Senior Officer Force F was ordered to be transferred from *Nelson* to *Duke of York* at Rosyth, and Syfret became Flag Officer Force H again with the

Force F title lapsing. He sailed from Scapa on 30 October in *Duke of York* with *Nelson, Rodney, Argonaut* and seven destroyers for Gibraltar.

In November 1942 the Allies at last went over to the offensive. In preparation for the invasion of North Africa, Operation Torch, Admiral Cunningham arrived in Gibraltar to become Allied Naval Commander of the Expeditionary Force and of the whole naval side of the great enterprise under the Allied Commander-in-Chief, General Eisenhower. Admiral Harwood retained command of the eastern basin from Cape Bon eastwards. All other naval forces in the western basin were to be within the Torch command. The British contribution would be concerned with the landings at Algiers by a mixed British and US force under American command, followed up by the British First Army. At Algiers and Oran the British naval forces deployed for their escort and supply would be the Eastern Task Force under command of Vice Admiral H. M. Burrough, and the Central Task Force commanded by Commodore T. H. Troubridge. Syfret with Force H, now consisting of three battleships, three aircraft carriers, three cruisers and seventeen destroyers, became responsible for covering the Algiers and Oran landings from attack by Italian warships. But this Force H was of a different nature to the earlier Force H. Instead of being a detached squadron with special terms of reference, it was, as already noted, now under the direct control of a commander-in-chief and was an integral part of the invading force;[2] its activities are recorded in that context.

The invading forces, 90,000 troops from America and 90,000 from Britain, launched their attacks on 8 November. Force H covered the arriving troop and supply convoys. In the first two months 437,000 Allied fighting men and 42,000 vehicles were landed. Four and a half million tons of shipping were involved, with total losses of 230,000 tons. Gibraltar was the hub of the whole operation. In January 1943 the force, comprising *Nelson, Rodney* and twelve destroyers, visited Algiers and then stayed in Oran for the rest of the month, chiefly to impress the local population with the spectacle of such a powerful Allied fleet. At the end of the month Syfret fell ill and Burrough temporarily relieved him. Vice Admiral A. U. Willis took over the command from Burrough on 4 March, with his flag in *Nelson*. In February Cunningham relinquished his title of Allied Naval Commander of the Expeditionary Force and resumed his former and more famous position as Commander-in-Chief Mediterranean. Harwood became Commander-in-Chief Levant, with his western boundary now moved further east to the Tunis–Tripoli frontier. This gave Cunningham control of the Tunisian coast, from whose ports part of the invasion force of Sicily would sail. In March Force H was ordered to return to

Gibraltar on indications that German capital ships now concentrated in north Norway might be intending a foray into the Atlantic.

Allied forces continued to drive the enemy out of the whole North African coastline and the two Inshore Squadrons from the east and west finally met at Bizerta. On 13 May the Axis armies in Africa surrendered. By 15 May minesweeping in the Sicilian Channel had cleared a passage to allow Cunningham to report that passage through the Mediterranean was clear. The first through convoy since the Tiger convoy of May 1941 arrived in Alexandria on 26 May 1943. The opening up of the Mediterranean meant that the long route round the Cape could be abandoned, releasing about a million tons of shipping. It was another turning point in the war. The lack of shipping had been a key factor in determining that no Second Front could take place in 1942. This obstacle had now been removed and made possible the invasion of the continent in June 1944. May 1943 also marked the turn of the Battle of the Atlantic in the Allies' favour; thirty-nine U-boats were destroyed in that month.

For the invasion of Sicily no chances were taken with the Italian fleet should it try to defend its country. Force H under Willis consisted of four battleships, *Nelson, Rodney, Warspite* and *Valiant,* and two aircraft carriers, *Formidable* and *Indomitable,* with two further battleships, *King George V* and *Howe,* in reserve but which also formed part of the bombarding force of two cruiser squadrons, totalling ten cruisers. A few days before the landing on 10 July Willis feinted to the south-west of Crete to keep the enemy guessing on the real whereabouts of the assault.

The Salerno landing, the first assault on the Italian mainland after the invasion of Sicily, was due to take place on 9 September. Before that plans had been made to effect the Italian surrender, which had already taken place. On 11 September Cunningham was able to signal the Admiralty, 'Be pleased to inform Their Lordships that the Italian battlefleet now lies at anchor under the guns of the fortress of Malta.' There was therefore no surface threat to the attack on Salerno, but naval gunfire support was required to assist the troops ashore. Every available ship including *Warspite* and *Valiant* bombarded the Germans and helped to neutralise the spearhead of their attack. During one bombardment *Warspite* was hit by a radio-controlled bomb which inflicted severe damage and many casualties.

With the Allied beach-head secure and the Mediterranean now clear of enemy surface forces, there was no further requirement for a strong covering force to protect Allied shipping. On 13 October 1943 Admiral Willis struck his flag and Force H and the Command activated three years earlier were finally disbanded.

Appendix 1: The Ships

DURING THE SQUADRON'S twenty-one-month existence, no fewer than ten capital ships (seven battleships and three battlecruisers), six aircraft carriers, twenty-three cruisers, eighty-three destroyers and two fast minelayers came under the operational command of Flag Officer Force H. Analysis of the 124 ships listed in Appendix 3 shows, as one would expect, that the hard-core elements of the squadron were present on the majority of occasions on which the force put to sea. *Ark Royal* took part in forty-one operations, *Renown* in thirty-five. The cruiser attachment, *Sheffield* (twenty-one) relieved by *Hermione* (seventeen), totalled thirty-eight. A further breakdown shows that forty-eight ships' names appear once only. These would have been ships deployed just for one particular operation, or one-way movements on passage to or from the Mediterranean Fleet. Of the remaining ships, in addition to the eleven ships forming the established force, those which took part in five or more operations were the capital ships *Hood*, *Valiant*, *Nelson* and *Malaya*; the carriers *Argus* and *Furious*; the cruisers *Arethusa* and *Enterprise*; and the destroyers *Duncan*, *Wishart*, *Active*, *Greyhound*, *Gallant*, *Hotspur*, *Velox*, *Wrestler*, *Isis*, *Griffin*, *Hesperus*, *Zulu*, *Sikh*, *Gurkha*, *Laforey*, *Lightning* and *Lance*. Of these, *Nelson* and *Malaya* served as flagships after *Renown*, and the last three L class destroyers as reliefs for the Fs. Apart also from the three Tribal class destroyers, the remaining destroyers were mostly from the local 13th Destroyer Flotilla.

The Admiral's flag was flown at sea on fifty-one occasions. *Hood* was flagship for the first five weeks before *Renown*, which was to become Somerville's favourite and longest-serving flagship and from which he attuned the squadron to its full efficiency. Her fast speed made her a good companion to *Ark Royal*, but fast steaming in heavy seas took its toll on some of her hull structure. While her lack of armour did not inhibit her in Mediterranean operations, it did cause her to be held back in the *Bismarck* action. As flagship she was a key member in formulating the special spirit in the squadron. *Nelson*'s time as flagship was short lived. After relieving *Renown* in July 1941 she was torpedoed two months later in the Halberd Malta convoy and had to return to Britain for repair. She was well suited to be a flagship, having served as fleet flagship for the Home Fleet, but her slower speed was a handicap when working with a carrier. This limitation also applied to *Malaya*, Somerville's next flagship and his least favoured. Not only had she poor endurance but she had not been modernised and her anti-aircraft armament was very weak, even though numbers of close-range Oerlikon guns were installed. Moreover her accommodation was inadequate to put up the Force H staff in reasonable conditions. The ship had been in action at the Battle of Jutland in 1916 and there remained a dent in the gundeck where she had been hit. She still retained the 6-inch gun battery each side between decks, designed to repel attacks by torpedo boat destroyers of the Imperial High Seas Fleet. Twenty-five years later the same guns repulsed torpedo attack, this time from aircraft, firing fused shell in barrage fire. The display was so impressive that a destroyer on the screen signalled admiringly about the 'wall of fire' from the ship.

Of the books written about individual ships and their wartime service, the most numerous have concerned *Ark Royal*, and tribute has been paid to her elsewhere in this book. Force H also relied on other carriers. At the other end of the scale was *Argus*, the world's first flush-decked aircraft carrier, which entered service in 1918. Operating with the force on Club Runs she carried no aircraft except the Hurricanes embarked for flying off to Malta. Once airborne the planes could not land back on again. Her top speed of 18 knots hindered Somerville in pursuing aggressive operations against the enemy, and prevented her from flying off Spitfires later in the war. He called her his pantechnicon, one of her main tasks being to carry crated fighters to Gibraltar and Takoradi in West Africa; but after *Ark Royal* was sunk she was given an operational role with eight Swordfish and two Fulmars embarked. Manoeuvring with the fleet, the small but doughty *Argus* with her flat top looked an incongruous figure against the other well-armed ships all endowed with generous topsides. This latter feature was especially prominent in *Eagle*, laid down in 1913 as a battleship for the Chilean Navy but purchased while still on the stocks and converted into an aircraft carrier. She flew off the first Spitfires to Malta and further reinforcements later in 1942, which were directly responsible for turning the tide against the Luftwaffe's attack on the island at its most desperate time. This gallant old ship was sunk in the last and hardest-fought Malta convoy in August 1942. *Furious* was another First World War construction. Laid down as a 'large light cruiser' in 1915 to carry two single 18-inch guns, she too was converted into a carrier. In the summer of 1941 she took part in several Club Runs, flying off Hurricanes for Malta. In comparison with *Ark Royal* these old ships might seem out of place, but their age did not put them in the second eleven. After the grievous capital-ship losses of December 1941, the Malta convoy of June 1942 had to rely on *Malaya*, *Eagle* and *Argus*, all of that earlier vintage.

Sheffield did not join Force H as a full member until October 1940. She did one Club Run in August but then returned to Britain for a refit. She was the first ship in the Navy to be fitted with air warning radar, and it was for this reason that she was sent to Force H. Among the ship's company there was considerable suspicion about the rotating aerials at the top of the mast, and the eight ratings of the RDF division (radio direction finding, as it was then known) were regarded as loafers by the seamen and as impostors by the communications ratings. But there was ready appreciation of their worth in *Ark Royal* (not fitted with radar) to which they were invited onboard with their specialist officer, a Canadian sub lieutenant RNVR. The ship was fitted with sonar and could be stationed on the screen if there was a shortage of destroyers. The cruiser's ability to look after herself ensured that she was given much detached work. Besides taking part in Club Runs in the Mediterranean she carried out patrols off the Azores and to investigate French ship movements. In the *Bismarck* action she suffered damage and casualties, as has been recounted (see pp. 91–5 above), and had to put up with torpedoes being fired at her by *Ark Royal*'s Swordfish. It was felt to be the last straw when one of the planes, having dropped its torpedo, sprayed the ship with its rear gun as it flew over the ship. However, a Swordfish contritely signalled 'Sorry for the kipper', and, in a much-appreciated gesture, on return to Gibraltar *Sheffield* invited the aircrews to drinks, saying 'all is forgiven and forgotten'.

Hermione relieved *Sheffield* after one year's service. She brought an increased air-defence capability to the force with radar of an improved performance and a heavier anti-aircraft armament. She was therefore well fitted to provide close supporting fire for *Ark Royal*, as well as fighter-direction information. Her gunfire capacity was also used to good effect when bombarding Pantelleria during the passage of the Halberd Malta convoy in September 1941. Sadly this good ship was sunk south of Crete in June 1942.

The destroyers of the 8th Destroyer Flotilla – *Faulknor* (leader), *Fortune*, *Fearless*, *Fury*, *Foresight*, *Foxhound*, *Firedrake* and *Forester* – are recorded in Appendix 3 as each escorting the main force on twenty or thirty occasions, less than the number of times the bigger ships went to sea. But this belies their amount of sea time; they were in fact the hardest-worked ships of the force. It became almost normal procedure for destroyers on return to harbour to refuel and proceed to sea again to carry out anti-submarine patrols in the Straits, or to escort convoys or for emergency or other local reasons, and these sorties are not recorded. It was established practice that the 8th Destroyer Flotilla and the local 13th Destroyer Flotilla should help each other out in fulfilling the many calls made on destroyers, for which there were never enough available. But whenever Somerville turned over the 8th DF for local work, he would always recall them for rest or repairs when necessary. *Duncan* was the leader of the 13th DF. The general routine on leaving harbour was for the destroyers to sail first to sweep ahead of the main body, and often as not to come in last after shepherding it back into harbour. At sea the high-speed steaming in fleet operations, especially when screening a carrier and changing station for flying operations, took its toll in machinery defects and run-down equipment. The engine-room staffs were praised by Somerville for keeping their ships going. Even so, at one time the force was reduced to three destroyers operational. In July 1941 the 8th DF celebrated the millionth mile steamed by them since the outbreak of war. The operational limitations of the short endurance of these ships and their need to refuel at sea have already been remarked upon, as has their inability to keep up with the big ships at high speed in heavy seas.

Relief of the F class by the L class commenced in June 1941. The Ls were new-construction larger ships and were more heavily armed, with either two twin 4.7-inch (*Laforey*, *Lightning*) or 4-inch (*Legion*, *Lance*) guns. *Laforey* was the leader of the 19th Destroyer Flotilla. To those serving in destroyers life was more agreeable and would not be changed for a more comfortable life on a bigger ship. The special small-ship camaraderie was enhanced by their berthing together at Gibraltar in the destroyer pens at the northern end of the harbour, well away from the bigger ships.

The merchant ships in the Malta convoys escorted by Force H were specially chosen. Some had a heavy-lift capability, as in the MT ships of the military convoys, but all were thoroughbreds of the British cargo fleet – 14–16 knot ships carrying 10,000–12,000 tons of cargo. Ships of the Clan, Glen, City and Blue Star lines came within this category. The ships were multi-loaded with a variety of stores so that if one ship was sunk there would not be a serious loss of any one type of cargo. The gun armament carried offered some close-range defence against air attack, and paravanes to protect against mines were fitted in a few ships. Heavily escorted on their outward voyage when carrying their valuable cargoes to Malta, these ships generally returned unescorted with empty holds, often repelling attack by E-boat, torpedo bomber or submarine. The determination and skill shown by their Masters were praised by Somerville.

This book is focused on Force H's activities, but mention must be made of other ships with which it was not directly involved but which played an important role. All submarine movements in the Mediterranean came under the control of the Commander-in-Chief, and although Somerville asked for submarines they did not form part of Force H. The 8th Submarine Flotilla, which included Dutch submarines, operated from Gibraltar but it was not until the end of March 1941 that the depot ship *Maidstone* was stationed there. The flotilla was in many ways comparable to Force H in that it divided its attention between defensive convoy escort in the Atlantic and offensive patrols in the western Mediterranean. In June 1941 the latter were given priority. Submarines patrolled off Messina and Palermo during the Substance and Halberd convoys, and also helped in the relief of Malta. There were frequent 'storing trips' run from Alexandria, and less often from Gibraltar, the first taking place in July 1940 when RAF personnel and 11 tons of stores were carried to the island.[1]

Another class of ship requested by Somerville was the fast minelayer. *Manxman* was used successfully on one minelaying expedition, and he saw other opportunities. A stock of mines equivalent to two ships' outfits was kept at Gibraltar. The high speed of which these ships were capable made them suitable for other operations, and he had in mind to use them to mount small raiding parties on Sardinia. Their cargo-carrying capacity in lieu of mines also fitted them well for delivering shipments of men and materials to Malta. Later in the war *Welshman*, disguised as a French light cruiser, was to make these runs.

Besides clandestine operations being carried out by submarine and fast minelayer to help relieve Malta, an occasional operation was planned for a merchant ship. In one instance, in conditions of greatest secrecy, SS *Parracombe*, a 9-knot single-screw coal-burning ship of 4700 tons, was loaded with twenty-one crated Hurricanes and sixty-eight UP projectiles and sailed from Britain in April 1941. It was considered an operation of great hazard and the specially selected crew had orders to scuttle to avoid capture. Spanish and French disguises were assumed as she passed along the North African coast; the dirtier and more tramplike she could look the better. She was to hug the African coast to avoid mines but although equipped with paravanes she hit a mine and sank on 2 May; eighteen survivors were landed at Bizerta.[2] Malta was in such desperate straits that these perilous missions had to be accepted.

SUMMARY OF FORCE H SHIP CASUALTIES

The following loss and damage to ships by enemy action were sustained during Force H operations:

Battleship

Nelson torpedoed and damaged in air attack on Halberd convoy, September 1941

Aircraft carrier

Ark Royal torpedoed and sunk by submarine when returning from Club Run, November 1941

Cruisers

Berwick damaged in surface action off Cape Spartivento, November 1940
Sheffield damaged in surface action against *Bismarck*, May 1941
Manchester torpedoed and damaged in air attack on Substance convoy, July 1941

Destroyers

Escort torpedoed and sunk by submarine in attack on Cagliari, July 1940
Hyperion mined and sunk on passage from Mediterranean Fleet, December 1940 (while under C-in-C Med. control)
Foresight bombed and damaged in Tiger convoy, May 1941
Fearless sunk and *Firedrake* damaged in air attack on Substance convoy, July 1941

Merchant ships

Empire Song mined and sunk, *New Zealand Star* mined and damaged in Tiger convoy, May 1941
Sydney Star torpedoed and damaged by E-boat in Substance convoy, July 1941
Imperial Star torpedoed and sunk in air attack on Halberd convoy, September 1941

Interestingly, these casualties do not reflect the predominant threat, which was perceived to be from air attack. While due credit for this must be given to the effectiveness of the fighter and AA gunnery defence, as well as to the handling of their ships by their captains and the force by Somerville, it was not until later in 1942, when the Luftwaffe was redeployed back to the area in strength from the Russian front, that the Gibraltar–Malta convoys became subject to more intensive air attack. But the sinkings by submarine confirmed that ever present threat at sea.

Appendix 2: Key Appointments

FLAG AND COMMANDING OFFICERS SERVING IN FORCE H

Flag Officer Force H	Vice Admiral Sir James Somerville KCB DSO
	Rear Admiral E. N. Syfret (from January 1942)
Chief of Staff	Captain E. G. Jeffrey
	Captain P. William-Powlett (from October 1941)
Staff Officer (Plans & Ops)	Commander A. W. Buzzard DSO
	Commander A. H. Thorold (from April 1941)

Flagship

Hood	Captain I. G. Glennie
Renown	Captain C. E. B. Simeon
	Captain R. R. McGrigor (from January 1941)
Nelson	Captain T. H. Troubridge
Malaya	Captain C. C. Coppinger DSC

Other key ships

Ark Royal	Captain C. S. Holland
	Captain L. E. H. Maund CBE (from March 1941)
Sheffield	Captain C. A. A. Larcom DSO
Hermione	Captain G. N. Oliver DSO

8th Destroyer Flotilla

Faulknor	D8 Captain A. F. de Salis DSO
Forester	Lieut. Comdr E. B. Tancock DSC
Foresight	Commander G. T. Lambert

	Commander J. S. C. Salter (from January 1941)
Firedrake	Lieut. Comdr S. H. Norris DSO DSC
Fortune	Commander E. A. Gibbs DSO
	Lieut. Comdr E. N. Sinclair (from November 1940)
	Lieut. Comdr R. D. A. S. Pankhurst (from October 1941)
Fearless	Commander I. H. R. Black
	Commander A. F. Pugsley (from December 1940)
Fury	Commander T. C. Robinson
Foxhound	Commander G. H. Peters DSC

19th Destroyer Flotilla

Laforey	D19 Captain R. M. J. Hutton
Lightning	Commander R. G. Stewart
Lance	Lieut. Comdr R. W. F. Northcott
Lively	Lieut. Comdr W. F. E. Hussey

SENIOR APPOINTMENTS JULY 1940–MARCH 1942

Admiralty

First Lord	A. V. Alexander
First Sea Lord	Admiral of the Fleet Sir Dudley Pound GCB GCVO
Vice Chief Naval Staff	actg Vice Admiral T. S. V. Phillips CB
	Vice Admiral H. R. Moore CVO DSO (from October 1941)

Commanders-in-Chief

Home Fleet	Admiral Sir Charles Forbes GCB DSO
	actg Admiral Sir John Tovey KCB DSO (from December 1940; Admiral from October 1942)

| Mediterranean | actg Admiral Sir Andrew Cunningham KCB DSO (Admiral from January 1941) |

Flag Officers

North Atlantic Station	Admiral Sir Dudley North KCVO CB CSI CMG
	Vice Admiral Sir George Edward-Collins KCB KCVO (from January 1941)
Malta	Vice Admiral Sir William Ford KBE CB

Attached Force H

For attack on Oran, July 1940	Vice Admiral L. V. Wells (Aircraft Carrier Squadron)
For Substance convoy, July 1941	Rear Admiral E. N. Syfret (18th Cruiser Squadron)
For Halberd convoy, Sep. 1941	actg Vice Admiral A. T. B. Curteis (2nd in Command Home Fleet)
	Rear Admiral H. M. Burrough (10th Cruiser Squadron)
	Rear Admiral E. N. Syfret (18th Cruiser Squadron)

Force M

| For attack on Dakar, Sep. 1940 | Vice Admiral Sir John Cunningham KCB MVO |

Appendix 3: Log of Force H Operations

DATE SAILED	AREA	SHIPS TAKING PART AND MISSION	CODENAME	PAGE
2.7.40	Med.	*Hood* (flag), *Valiant, Resolution, Ark Royal, Arethusa, Enterprise, Faulknor, Foxhound, Fearless, Forester, Foresight, Escort, Keppel, Active, Wrestler, Vidette, Vortigern* – action against French Fleet at Oran	Catapult	28
5.7.40	Med.	Same force less *Resolution* – second attack against *Dunkerque*	Lever	32
8.7.40	Med.	*Hood* (flag), *Valiant, Resolution, Ark Royal, Arethusa, Enterprise, Delhi, Faulknor, Fearless, Forester, Foxhound, Escort, Wrestler, Velox, Vortigern, Active, Douglas* – air attack on Cagliari as diversion for Malta–Alexandria convoy operation (not carried out, risk of putting *Ark Royal* out of action not justified)		39
23.7.40	Atlantic	*Ark Royal, Enterprise, Faulknor, Foresight, Forester, Escapade* – attack on merchant shipping in Le Verdun Roads, Gironde area (operation subsequently cancelled)		41
31.7.40	Med.	Group 1: *Hood* (flag), *Ark Royal, Enterprise, Faulknor, Foxhound, Foresight*; Group 2: *Valiant, Resolution, Argus, Arethusa, Forester, Hotspur, Greyhound, Gallant, Escapade, Encounter, Velox* – air attack by Group 1 on Cagliari; Group 2 to fly off twelve Hurricanes from *Argus* for Malta – *Enterprise* detached to transmit confusing radio messages.	Hurry / Spark	42

DATE SAILED	AREA	SHIPS TAKING PART AND MISSION	CODENAME	PAGE
4.8.40	Atlantic	*Hood* (flag), *Valiant, Argus, Arethusa, Faulknor, Foresight, Forester, Foxhound, Escapade* – sailed for UK		43
10.8.40		Flag FO(H) transferred to *Renown*		43
16.8.40	Atlantic	*Ark Royal, Enterprise, Greyhound, Gallant, Hotspur, Encounter, Wrestler* – to rendezvous *Renown* (flag), *Bedouin, Punjabi, Mashona, Tartar* from Scapa arriving Gibraltar 20 August		44
25.8.40	Atlantic	*Renown* (flag), *Ark Royal, Enterprise, Gallant, Hotspur, Griffin, Velox, Encounter, Greyhound, Vidette* – for exercises and to rendezvous Mediterranean Fleet reinforcements		44
30.8.40	Med.	*Renown* (flag), *Ark Royal, Sheffield, Faulknor, Fortune, Fury, Foresight, Firedrake, Encounter, Wishart, Velox*, Force F: *Valiant, Illustrious, Coventry, Calcutta, Gallant, Greyhound, Hotspur, Griffin, Nubian, Mohawk, Janus, Hero* – to pass reinforcements (Force F) through to eastern Mediterranean	Hats	44
6.9.40	Atlantic	*Barham, Resolution, Ark Royal, Faulknor, Fury, Fortune, Forester, Greyhound, Inglefield, Eclipse, Escapade, Echo* – to join Force M for attack on Dakar	Menace	46
11.9.40	Atlantic	*Renown* (flag), *Griffin, Vidette, Velox* – to intercept French cruisers if sailing beyond Casablanca		46
17.9.40	Atlantic	*Renown* (flag) and destroyers – to patrol south-west of Straits to intercept French force located by patrols in the Straits		47
24.9.40	Atlantic	*Renown* (flag) and four destroyers – to clear harbour during French air attack on Gibraltar and patrol to westward		49

DATE SAILED	AREA	SHIPS TAKING PART AND MISSION	CODENAME	PAGE
29.9.40	Atlantic	*Renown* (flag), *Hotspur, Encounter, Gallant, Firedrake* – to intercept *Richelieu* but later amended to patrol off Azores against capture by troops in two German merchant ships		51
30.9.40	Atlantic	*Ark Royal* left Freetown for UK carrying out recce of Dakar en route. Short refit at Liverpool, returning to Gibraltar 6.11.40		54
12.10.40	Atlantic	*Renown* (flag), *Vidette, Gallant, Griffin, Wishart* – to be clear of Gibraltar in anticipation of French reprisal raid and patrol to westward		51
19.10.40	Atlantic	*Faulknor, Forester, Fury, Foresight* returned – to Gibraltar after the Dakar expedition		52
27.10.40	Atlantic	*Sheffield* – to patrol off Azores to intercept German troop transports from Biscay ports should an invasion of the islands be attempted		52
31.10.40	Atlantic	*Renown* (flag), *Barham, Fortune, Firedrake, Fury, Greyhound* – on report of sighting of five French destroyers		53
6.11.40	Atlantic	*Renown* and destroyers – to cover convoys against attack by *Admiral Scheer*		54
7.11.40	Med.	*Ark Royal* (flag), *Sheffield, Faulknor, Fortune, Fury, Foxhound, Forester, Firedrake, Duncan, Isis*; Mediterranean Fleet reinforcements: *Barham, Berwick, Glasgow, Greyhound, Gallant, Griffin* – to pass reinforcements to eastern Mediterranean	Coat	54
15.11.40	Med.	*Renown* (flag), *Ark Royal, Argus, Sheffield, Despatch, Faulknor, Fury, Fortune, Forester, Firedrake, Foxhound, Duncan, Wishart* – to fly off twelve Hurricanes from *Argus* for Malta. Solo passage by *Newcastle* to Malta during operation	White	56

DATE SAILED	AREA	SHIPS TAKING PART AND MISSION	CODENAME	PAGE
22.11.40	Straits	*Despatch, Faulknor, Forester* – to intercept French merchant ship	Ration	57
25.11.40	Med.	*Renown* (flag), *Ark Royal, Manchester, Despatch, Southampton, Sheffield, Faulknor, Fury, Firedrake, Forester, Kelvin, Jaguar, Encounter, Wishart*; Convoy MT ships: *New Zealand Star* (to Alexandria); *Clan Forbes, Clan Fraser* (to Malta). *Manchester* and *Southampton* with embarked troops and RAF personnel for Alexandria. Action off Cape Spartivento	Collar	58
5.12.40	Atlantic	*Sheffield* – to patrol off Azores		
12.12.40	Straits	*Faulknor (D8), Forester, Fury, Isis* – to intercept French convoy	Ration	62
14.12.40	Atlantic	*Renown* (flag), *Ark Royal, Faulknor, Fury, Forester, Isis, Encounter, Duncan* – to patrol off Azores on report of German expedition about to leave Bordeaux		62
17.12.40	Atlantic	*Berwick* – to maintain Azores patrol		
20.12.40	Med.	*Renown* (flag), *Ark Royal, Sheffield, Faulknor, Forester, Fury, Firedrake, Fortune, Foxhound, Duncan, Encounter, Isis, Wishart, Jaguar* – to support westbound passage from Malta of *Malaya, Hyperion, Ilex, Hero, Hasty, Hereward,* SS *Clan Forbes, Clan Fraser*	Hide	62
25.12.40	Atlantic	*Renown* (flag), *Ark Royal, Sheffield, Faulknor, Fortune, Firedrake, Foxhound, Duncan, Wishart, Hero, Hereward* – on report of convoy WS 5A being attacked by *Hipper*		63

1941

DATE SAILED	AREA	SHIPS TAKING PART AND MISSION	CODENAME	PAGE
1.1.41	Straits	*Bonaventure, Duncan, Jaguar, Foxhound, Firedrake, Hero* – to intercept French merchant ships	Ration	64

DATE SAILED	AREA	SHIPS TAKING PART AND MISSION	CODENAME	PAGE
7.1.41	Med.	Group 1: *Renown* (flag), *Malaya, Ark Royal, Sheffield, Faulknor, Firedrake, Forester, Fury, Foxhound, Fortune, Jaguar*; Group 2: *Bonaventure, Duncan, Hereward, Hasty, Hero*; Convoy MT ships: SS *Essex* (to Malta); SS *Clan MacDonald, Clan Cumming, Empire Song* (to Piraeus) – to pass convoy and Group 2 to eastern Mediterranean	Excess	71
31.1.41	Med.	*Renown* (flag), *Malaya, Ark Royal, Sheffield, Duncan, Isis, Encounter, Jupiter, Fearless, Foxhound, Foresight, Fury, Firedrake, Jersey* – for attack on Tirso Dam (1) and bombardment of Genoa (2) (bombardment abandoned)	Picket (1) Result (2)	73
6.2.41	Med.	*Renown* (flag), *Malaya, Ark Royal, Sheffield, Fearless, Foxhound, Foresight, Fury, Encounter, Jersey, Duncan, Isis, Firedrake, Jupiter* – bombardment of Genoa	Grog	73
12.2.41	Atlantic	*Renown* (flag), *Ark Royal, Sheffield, Wishart, Jersey, Foxhound, Firedrake, Fury* – to assist convoy HG 53 and escort convoy WS 6		78
3.3.41	Med.	*Ark Royal, Fearless, Fortune, Duncan* – for flying exercises		
8.3.41	Atlantic	*Renown* (flag), *Ark Royal, Arethusa, Velox, Wrestler* – towards Canary Islands to support convoy SL 67		79
24.3.41	Atlantic	*Renown* (flag), *Ark Royal, Foresight, Forester, Fortune* – for Bay of Biscay patrol		80
29.3.41	Med.	*Sheffield, Faulknor, Fury, Fearless, Forester* – to intercept French convoy carrying war material	Ration	80
1.4.41	Med.	*Renown* (flag), *Ark Royal, Faulknor, Foresight, Fury, Fortune* – to fly off twelve Hurricanes for Malta	Winch	81

DATE SAILED	AREA	SHIPS TAKING PART AND MISSION	CODENAME	PAGE
4.4.41	Atlantic	*Renown* (flag), *Ark Royal, Furious, Sheffield, Faulknor, Fearless, Fortune, Foresight* – to clear harbour from French retaliatory attack and to exchange aircraft between carriers		81
7.4.41	Atlantic	*Renown* (flag), *Ark Royal, Sheffield, Fiji, Faulknor, Fearless, Foresight* – for Bay of Biscay patrol		82
24.4.41	Med.	*Renown* (flag), *Ark Royal, Sheffield, Faulknor, Fortune, Fearless, Fury, Foresight* (1); Force S: *Dido, Abdiel, Kelly, Kipling, Kelvin, Kashmir, Jersey, Jackal* (2) – to fly off twenty-three Hurricanes for Malta and Force S passage to eastern Mediterranean	Dunlop (1) Salient (2)	82
5.5.41	Med.	*Renown* (flag), *Ark Royal, Fiji, Sheffield, Naiad, Gloucester, Kashmir, Kipling, Faulknor, Forester, Foresight, Fortune, Fearless, Velox, Fury, Havelock, Hesperus, Harvester,* to r/v convoy *Queen Elizabeth,* SS *Clan Campbell, Clan Lamont, Clan Chattan, Empire Song, New Zealand Star* – passage of convoy to Alexandria	Tiger	84
19.5.41	Med.	*Renown* (flag), *Ark Royal, Furious, Sheffield, Faulknor, Fearless, Foxhound, Fury, Brilliant, Hesperus* – to fly off forty-eight Hurricanes for Malta	Splice	87
24.5.41	Atlantic	*Renown* (flag), *Ark Royal, Sheffield, Faulknor, Forester, Foresight, Foxhound, Fury, Hesperus* – to support convoy WS 8B, thence to intercept *Bismarck*		89
5.6.41	Med.	*Renown* (flag), *Furious, Ark Royal, Faulknor, Foxhound, Foresight, Forester, Fearless, Fury* – to fly off forty-three Hurricanes for Malta	Rocket	97

DATE SAILED	AREA	SHIPS TAKING PART AND MISSION	CODENAME	PAGE
7.6.41	Atlantic	*Renown* (flag), *Ark Royal*, *Furious*, *Sheffield*, *Faulknor*, *Foxhound*, *Foresight*, *Forester*, *Fearless*, *Fury* – to the westward to clear harbour in anticipation of French reprisal bombing attack		97
13.6.41	Med.	*Renown* (flag), *Ark Royal*, *Victorious*, *Faulknor*, *Fearless*, *Foresight*, *Forester*, *Foxhound*, *Hesperus*, *Wishart* – to fly off forty-seven Hurricanes for Malta	Tracer	97
15.6.41	Atlantic	*Victorious* and 8th DF destroyers – *Victorious* to return UK, destroyers returning Gibraltar		97
22.6.41	Atlantic	*Faulknor*, *Fearless*, *Foxhound*, *Forester*, *Fury* – to westward to intercept enemy supply ship		97
26.6.41	Med.	*Renown* (flag), *Ark Royal*, *Hermione*, *Faulknor*, *Fury*, *Forester*, *Legion*, *Lance* – to fly off fifteen Hurricanes for Malta	Railway Phase 1	97
28.6.41	Med.	*Renown* (flag), *Ark Royal*, *Furious*, *Hermione*, *Fearless*, *Foxhound*, *Faulknor*, *Fury*, *Forester*, *Legion*, *Lance* – to fly off twenty-five Hurricanes for Malta	Railway Phase 2	97
1.7.41	Atlantic	*Faulknor*, *Fearless*, *Forester*, *Lance*, *Legion* – to escort convoy OG 66 to Gibraltar		
1.7.41	Atlantic	*Hermione* – to intercept possible German raider or supply ship		
4.7.41	Atlantic	*Furious*, *Hermione*, *Wishart*, *Fury*, *Lance*, *Legion* – to r/v *Royal Sovereign* for onward escort to UK		

DATE SAILED	AREA	SHIPS TAKING PART AND MISSION	CODENAME	PAGE
11.7.41	Med.	*Ark, Royal, Foxhound, Fearless, Foresight, Eridge* – for exercises and flying training		
21.7.41	Med.	*Renown* (flag), *Nelson, Ark Royal, Hermione, Faulknor, Fearless, Foxhound, Firedrake, Foresight, Fury, Forester, Duncan*; Force X: *Edinburgh, Manchester, Arethusa, Manxman, Cossack, Maori, Sikh, Lightning, Nestor, Eridge, Avon Vale, Farndale*; Convoy: SS *Melbourne Star, Durham, Port Chalmers, Sydney Star, City of Pretoria* – passage of Force X and convoy to Malta	Substance	100
27.7.41		Flag FO(H) transferred to *Nelson*		106
30.7.41	Med.	*Nelson* (flag), *Renown, Ark Royal, Faulknor, Foresight, Fury, Foxhound, Cossack, Maori, Nestor, Encounter, Eridge*; Force X: *Hermione, Arethusa, Manxman, Lightning, Sikh* – passage of Force X to Malta with 1746 Army personnel ex-*Manchester* and SS *Leinster*	Style	104
8.8.41	Atlantic	*Renown, Cossack, Maori, Sikh, Lightning* – return to UK		106
20.8.41	Med.	*Nelson* (flag), *Ark Royal, Hermione, Nestor, Encounter, Foresight, Fury, Forester* – to make diversion for minelaying operation by *Manxman* by carrying out incendiary attacks on cork woods in Sardinia	Mincemeat	106
8.9.41	Med.	*Ark Royal* (flag), *Gurkha, Lively, Lance, Forester* – to fly off twenty-six Hurricanes to Malta	Status 1	107
10.9.41	Med.	*Nelson* (flag), *Ark Royal, Furious, Hermione, Legion, Foresight, Forester, Lively, Lance, Zulu, Gurkha* – to fly off twenty-three Hurricanes to Malta	Status 2	107

DATE SAILED	AREA	SHIPS TAKING PART AND MISSION	CODENAME	PAGE
24.9.41	Med.	Group 1: *Nelson* (flag), *Ark Royal, Hermione, Cossack, Zulu, Foresight, Laforey, Lightning*; Group 2: *Prince of Wales, Rodney, Kenya, Edinburgh, Sheffield, Euryalus, Duncan, Gurkha, Legion, Lance, Lively, Oribi, Isaac Sweers, Piorun, Garland, Fury, Farndale, Heythrop*; Convoy: HMS *Breconshire*, SS *Clan MacDonald, Clan Ferguson, Ajax, Imperial Star, City of Lincoln, Rowallan Castle, Dunedin Star, City of Calcutta* – passage of convoy to Malta	Halberd	108
16.10.41	Med.	*Rodney* (flag), *Ark Royal, Hermione, Cossack, Zulu, Sikh, Legion, Foresight, Forester, Fury*; Force K: *Aurora, Penelope, Lance, Lively* – to fly off eleven Albacores and two Swordfish for Malta and passage of Force K to eastern Mediterranean	Callboy	116
10.41		Flag FO(H) transferred to *Malaya*		116
10.11.41	Med.	*Malaya* (flag), *Ark Royal, Argus, Hermione, Laforey, Lightning, Legion, Zulu, Gurkha, Sikh, Isaac Sweers* – to fly off thirty-seven Hurricanes for Malta	Perpetual	117
16.11.41	Med.	*Deptford, Wild Swan, Pentstemon, Convolvulus, Rhododendron, Samphire, Marigold*; Convoy: *Brown Ranger*, SS *Blair Atholl, Baron Newlands, Shuna, Cisnerus, Ottinge* – dummy convoy sailed as diversion, ships returning to Gibraltar independently	Chieftain	120
16.11.41	Atlantic	*Nelson, Zulu, Sikh, Gurkha, Argus, Hermione, Laforey, Legion, Isaac Sweers, Lightning* – first four named ships to return to UK		120
11.12.41	Med.	*Sikh, Maori, Legion, Isaac Sweers* – to join Mediterranean Fleet		120

DATE SAILED	AREA	SHIPS TAKING PART AND MISSION	CODENAME	PAGE
19.12.41	Med.	*Malaya* (flag), *Laforey, Foxhound, Hesperus, Whitehall, Nestor, Fortune, Arrow, Campbeltown, Zulu, Gurkha* – for practice firings		120
20.12.41	Med.	*Argus, Hermione, Laforey, Zulu, Gurkha, Nestor, Arrow, Foxhound, Whitehall, Hesperus, Fortune* – for exercises		120
22.12.41	Med.	*Dido, Gurkha, Zulu, Nestor, Foxhound, Arrow* – to Malta		120

1942

10.1.42		Rear Admiral E. N. Syfret takes command Force H		123
22.1.42	Atlantic	*Hermione* – Azores patrol		
8.2.42	Atlantic	*Malaya* (flag), *Hermione, Laforey, Lightning, Blankney, Croome, Exmoor, Westcott, Active, Anthony* – return to UK to escort troop convoy WS 16		123
17.2.42	Atlantic	*Malaya* (flag), *Eagle, Hermione, Laforey, Lightning, Active, Duncan* – returned to Gibraltar 23.2.42 after escorting convoy WS 16		123
27.2.42	Med.	*Malaya* (flag), *Eagle, Argus, Hermione, Laforey, Lightning, Duncan, Whitehall, Active, Blankney, Croome, Wishart* – for Club Run, mission aborted		123
6.3.42	Med.	Repeat operation 27.2.42 (less *Duncan*, but with *Exmoor* and *Anthony*) – to fly off fifteen Spitfires to Malta		124

DATE SAILED	AREA	SHIPS TAKING PART AND MISSION	CODENAME	PAGE
1.4.42	Atlantic	*Malaya* (flag), *Hermione, Laforey, Lightning, Active, Anthony, Duncan* – for attack on Diego Suarez, Madagascar. <u>Force H title lapsed on sailing from Gibraltar.</u>	Ironclad	124

Source References

Chapter 1: The Formation of Force H

1   Roskill, *War at Sea*, vol. I, p. 242
2   Macintyre, *Fighting Admiral*, p. 85
3   ADM 1/19180, Admiralty Message 1724/28/6/40
4   Simpson (ed.), *Somerville Papers*, p. 123
5   ADM 1/19180, Admiralty Message 1152/30/12/40
6   Simpson (ed.), *Somerville Papers*, p. 285

Chapter 2: Gibraltar

1   Hughes and Athanassios, *Strong as the Rock of Gibraltar*, p. 27
2   *ibid.*, p. 147
3   *ibid.*, p. 30
4   Benady, *Royal Navy at Gibraltar*, p. 165
5   *ibid.*, p. 204

Chapter 3: The Attack on the French Fleet

1   Simpson (ed.), *Somerville Papers*, p. 96
2   Benady, *Royal Navy at Gibraltar*, p. 154
3   Simpson (ed.), *Somerville Papers*, p. 94
4   Churchill, *Second World War*, vol. II, p. 209
5   Simpson (ed.), *Somerville Papers*, p. 97
6   *ibid.*, pp. 105–6
7   Journal, Midshipman R. Macdonald, HMS *Valiant*
8   Gilbert, *Finest Hour*, p. 639
9   *ibid.*, p. 988
10   Churchill, *Second World War*, vol. II, p. 202
11   *ibid.*, p. 212
12   *ibid.*, p. 207

Chapter 4: Naval Enterprise and Political Confusion

1   Roskill, *War at Sea*, vol. I, p. 295
2   Macintyre, *Fighting Admiral*, p. 76
3   Simpson (ed.), *Somerville Papers*, p. 125

4   *ibid.*, p. 152
5   *ibid.*, pp. 152–3
6   Roskill, *War at Sea*, vol. I, p. 315
7   *ibid.*, p. 319
8   *ibid.*, p. 159
9   Simpson (ed.), *Somerville Papers*, p. 145
10   ADM 1/19180, First Sea Lord minute 8.10.40 in M.019598/40
11   Brodhurst, *Churchill's Anchor*, pp. 170–1
12   Marder, *Operation Menace*, p. 260
13   Simpson (ed.), *Somerville Papers*, p. 188
14   *ibid.*, p. 172
15   *ibid.*, p. 172
16   *ibid.*, p. 149
17   Roskill, *War at Sea*, vol. I, p. 275
18   Simpson (ed.), *Somerville Papers*, p. 181
19   Roskill, *War at Sea*, vol. I, p. 298
20   Simpson (ed.), *Somerville Papers*, p. 187
21   Simpson (ed.), *Cunningham Papers*, vol. I, pp. 204, 208
22   Brodhurst, *Churchill's Anchor*, p. 174
23   Simpson (ed.), *Somerville Papers*, p. 208
24   Simpson (ed.), *Cunningham Papers*, vol. I, p. 208; Cunningham of
       Hyndhope, *Sailor's Odyssey*, p. 293
25   Simpson (ed.), *Somerville Papers*, p. 220
26   Marder, *From the Dreadnought to Scapa Flow*, vol. II, p. 75
27   Massie, *Castles of Steel*, p. 145
28   Simpson (ed.), *Somerville Papers*, p. 228
29   Roskill, *War at Sea*, vol. I, p. 420
30   Simpson (ed.), *Somerville Papers*, p. 242
31   *ibid.*, p. 202
32   *ibid.*, p. 256
33   Macintyre, *Fighting Admiral*, p. 106
34   Simpson (ed.), *Somerville Papers*, p. 285
35   *ibid.*, p. 216
36   *ibid.*, p. 222
37   Woods, *Wings at Sea*, p. 8

Chapter 5: In the Ascendant

1   *Naval Staff History: Selected Bombardments*, p. 28
2   Simpson (ed.), *Somerville Papers*, p. 243

3   Jellicoe, *Grand Fleet 1914–1916*, p. 180

4   Roskill, *War at Sea*, vol. I, p. 392

5   Bassett, *HMS Sheffield*, pp. 85–6

6   Gilbert, *Finest Hour*, p. 1066

7   Simpson (ed.), *Somerville Papers*, p. 259

8   Macintyre, *Fighting Admiral*, p. 121

9   Simpson (ed.), *Somerville Papers*, p. 263

10   Cunningham of Hyndhope, *Sailor's Odyssey*, p. 263

11   Roskill, *War at Sea*, vol. I, p. 446

12   Simpson (ed.), *Somerville Papers*, p. 267

13   Woods, *Wings at Sea*, p. 93

14   ADM 199/657, report 26.5.41, pp. 32–9

15   Woods, *Wings at Sea*, pp. 94–5

16   Macintyre, *Fighting Admiral*, p. 119

17   Roskill, *War at Sea*, vol. I, p. 438

18   *ibid.*, p. 418

19   Simpson (ed.), *Somerville Papers*, p. 266

Chapter 6: At Full Stretch

1   Simpson (ed.), *Somerville Papers*, p. 303

2   Macintyre, *Fighting Admiral*, p. 154

3   Journal, Midshipman R. P. Dannreuther, HMS *Laforey*

4   Journal, Midshipman C. D. V. Nicoll, HMS *Nelson*

5   Thompson, *Imperial War Museum Book of War at Sea*, p. 124

6   Simpson (ed.), *Somerville Papers*, p. 335

7   *Gibraltar Chronicle*, 15, 17 November 1941

8   ADM 156, Case 6159, vol. I

Chapter 7: Exercising Sea Power

1   Simpson (ed.), *Cunningham Papers*, vol. I, p. 546

2   Roskill, *War at Sea*, vol. I, p. 274

3   *ibid.*, p. 242

4   Marder, *From Dreadnought to Scapa Flow*, p. 27

5   Simpson (ed.), *Cunningham Papers*, vol. I, p. 555

Epilogue

1   Naval Historical Branch, MOD, Admiralty Message 1636/24/5/42

2   Roskill, *War at Sea*, vol. II, pp. 313–15

Appendix 1: The Ships

1   *Naval Staff History: Second World War, Submarines*, vol. II
2   ADM 199/1810

Acknowledgements

TWO SOURCES IN particular have provided the basis for this book. First and foremost is *The Somerville Papers* edited by Michael Simpson and commissioned by the Navy Records Society, to both of whom I give recognition in the Preface; and I thank the latter and the book's publisher Scolar Press for allowing me to quote extracts. The second book, *Fighting Admiral* by Captain Donald Macintyre DSO DSC, recording the life of Admiral Somerville, has also been of great value and I thank HarperCollins Publishers for raising no objection to my quoting from it. I also thank HMSO for permission to quote from *The Official History of the War at Sea*, volumes I and II; Conway Maritime Press for permission to quote from *Wings at Sea*; and Ashgate Publishing Group for permission to quote from *The Cunningham Papers*.

There are other books, noted in the text as Source References, which I acknowledge. Not least of these are the papers in The National Archives, now clear of copyright, which have provided a substantial contribution to the writing of the book, in particular Admiral Somerville's reports of proceedings.

From the outset I have been impressed by the kindness shown me and the help and guidance so readily given. I am grateful to Commander Alastair Wilson, Secretary of the *Naval Review*, and Captain Richard Woodman for giving me a steer in the early days; to Michael Simpson and Captain Christopher Page, Head of the Naval Historical Branch in the Ministry of Defence, for making additional information available to me; and to John Somerville CB CBE, Captain Barrie Kent and Charles Dannreuther for reading and commenting on my first draft. I also wish to thank for their helpful contributions my Force H shipmate Captain David Nicoll (ex *Nelson* and *Malaya*), and Commander Peter Meryon DSC (ex *Wrestler*), Commander Felix Neville-Towle DSC (ex *Forester*), Lieutenant Commander Henry Nash (ex Swordfish TAG), Commander Donald MacQueen (ex Swordfish pilot); Lady Seccombe for the memoirs of her late husband, then Sub Lieutenant Hugh Seccombe RNVR and serving in *Faulknor*; Captain and Mrs Bryan Salwey for the taped reminiscences of the latter's father, then Commander A. H. Thorold serving as Staff Officer (Plans) to Admiral Somerville from April 1941; and to the Naval Historical Collectors and Research Association for extracts from the late Vice Admiral Sir Roderick Macdonald's journal as midshipman (ex *Valiant*). And for consenting to write the Foreword to this book I thank

Admiral of the Fleet Sir Henry Leach GCB DL, a long-time friend and fellow gunnery officer whose father commanded the battleship *Prince of Wales* throughout 1941.

In pursuit of information from their archives I have been grateful for the help and interest shown by the staffs of The National Archives, the National Maritime Museum, the Imperial War Museum, the Royal Naval Museum, the Fleet Air Arm Museum, Firepower: the Royal Artillery Museum, the Royal Air Force Museum, the Garrison Library Gibraltar, the National War Museum Malta GC, the Second World War Experience Centre, and Farnham town library.

On the home front I must record my gratitude to my daughter-in-law Catherine for her help with the typing, for which I also wish to thank Sharon Thayer; and to my sons Richard for relieving me of my computer-generated frustrations and Charles for casting an academic eye over my literary efforts; and especially to my wife Elizabeth for her continued support and encouragement.

On some points of detail, the sources conflict. I have chosen what I consider to be the most pertinent and accurate versions. I take responsibility for any errors and omissions.

Bibliography

PUBLISHED WORKS

Bassett, R., *HMS Sheffield*, Arms & Armour Press, 1988

Benady, T., *The Royal Navy at Gibraltar*, Maritime Books, 1992

Brodhurst, R., *Churchill's Anchor: Admiral of the Fleet Sir Dudley Pound*, Leo Cooper, 2000

Careless, R., *Battleship Nelson*, Arms & Armour Press, 1985

Churchill, W. S., *The Second World War*, vol. II: *Their Finest Hour*, vol. III: *The Grand Alliance*, Cassell, 1949 and 1950

Cunningham of Hyndhope, Viscount, *A Sailor's Odyssey*, Hutchinson, 1951

Gilbert, M., *Finest Hour*, Heinemann, 1983

Hill, J. R. (ed.), *Oxford Illustrated History of the Royal Navy*, Oxford University Press, 1995

Hughes, Q. and Athanassios, M., *Strong as the Rock of Gibraltar*, Exchange Publications, 1995

Jameson, W., *Ark Royal 1939–41*, Rupert Hart-Davis, 1957

Jellicoe, Viscount, *The Grand Fleet 1914–1916*, Cassell, 1919

Jenkins, R., *Churchill*, Macmillan, 2001

Kemp, P., *The Admiralty Regrets: British Warship Losses of the 20th Century*, Sutton, 1999

Macintyre, D. G., *Fighting Admiral*, Evans Brothers, 1961

McCart, N., *Three Ark Royals, 1938–99*, Fan Publications, 1999

Marder, A., *From the Dreadnought to Scapa Flow*, vols II and IV, Oxford University Press, 1959 and 1969

Marder, A., *Operation Menace: The Dakar Expedition and the Dudley North Affair*, Oxford University Press, 1976

Massie, R. K., *Castles of Steel*, Jonathan Cape, 2004

Naval Staff History: The Second World War, Submarines, vol. II, HMSO, 1955

Naval Staff History: Selected Bombardments (Mediterranean 1940–41), HMSO, 1954

Ray, J., *The Second World War*, Cassell, 1999

Roskill, S. W., *The War at Sea*, vols I and II, HMSO, 1954 and 1956

Simpson, M. (ed.), *The Cunningham Papers*, vol. I, Ashgate/Navy Records Society, 1999

Simpson, M. (ed.), *The Somerville Papers*, Scolar/Navy Records Society, 1995

Simpson, M., 'Force H and British Strategy in the Western Mediterranean 1939–42', *The Mariner's Mirror*, vol. 83 no. 1, February 1997

Smith, P. C., *Hit First Hit Hard* (HMS Renown), William Kimber, 1979

Stephen, M., *The Fighting Admirals*, Leo Cooper, 1991

Thompson, J., *Imperial War Museum Book of the War at Sea*, Sidgwick & Jackson, 1996

Woodman, R., *Malta Convoys*, John Murray, 2000

Woods, G. A., *Wings at Sea*, Conway Maritime Press, 1985

Von der Porten, E. P., *German Navy in World War Two*, Pan Books, 1970

DOCUMENTS

National Archives

ADM 1 series including:

/19180 – Formation and policy of Force H

/19182 – Relationship FOCNAS and FO(H)

ADM 199 series including:

Somerville's reports of proceedings

/391 – July–August 1940

/392 – September–December 1940

/656 – January–May 1941

/657 – May–December 1941

Index

Page references in *italics* refer to maps.